COLLEGE
— WITHOUT —
COMMUNISM

COLLEGE —WITHOUT— COMMUNISM

HOW CHRISTIANS CAN RECLAIM TRUTH IN HIGHER EDUCATION

DR. KENT INGLE
JOSHUA LISEC

Southeastern University Press
Lakeland, FL

College Without Communism copyright © 2025 by Kent Ingle and Joshua Lisec

All rights reserved. No part of this publication may be reproduced, distributed, or transmitted in any form or by any means, including photocopying, recording, or other electronic or mechanical methods, without the prior written permission of the publisher, except in the case of brief quotations embodied in critical reviews and certain other noncommercial uses permitted by copyright law. For permission requests, write to the publisher at the address below.

Southeastern University Press
1000 Longfellow Boulevard
Lakeland, Florida 33801
United States of America
(800) 500-8760

Publisher's Cataloging-In-Publication Data

Names: Ingle, Kent, 1962- author. | Lisec, Joshua, author.
Title: College without communism : how Christians can reclaim truth in higher education / Dr. Kent Ingle [and] Joshua Lisec.
Description: Lakeland, FL : Southeastern University Press, [2025] | Includes bibliographical references.
Identifiers: ISBN: 9798993115412 (hardcover) | 9798993115405 (softcover) | 9798993115429 (ebook) | 9798993115436 (audiobook)
Subjects: LCSH: Education, Higher--Religious aspects--Christianity. | Christian education--United States. | Universities and colleges--Philosophy. | Church and college--United States. | Christian universities and colleges--United States.
Classification: LCC: LB2328.2 .I54 2025 | DDC: 378.001--dc23

Special discounts for bulk sales are available.

Please contact seupublications@seu.edu.

Praise for *College Without Communism*

"College education has become rotten to its core. But it doesn't have to be. Higher education began as a Christian endeavor, and in *College Without Communism*, Kent explains how we can undo the damage and restore college as it is meant to be."
— Charlie Kirk, Co-Founder, Turning Point USA *(Rest in Peace)*

"Marxist Vladimir Lenin said, 'Give me four years to teach the children and the seed I have sown will never be uprooted.' In *College Without Communism*, Dr. Ingle and Joshua show why Lenin said that—and what we can do about communist indoctrination in American higher education before it is too late."
— Benjamin S. Carson, Sr., MD
Founder and Chairman, American Cornerstone Institute
17th United States Secretary of the Department of Housing and Urban Development
Emeritus Professor of Neurosurgery, Johns Hopkins Medicine

"Communism is everywhere. The ideology didn't die after the fall of the Soviet Union; it mutated. Dr. Kent Ingle clocks the new version—'the woke mind virus'—as it overtakes academia. But he shows a new way forward for all Christian parents to find higher education options that support our sons' and daughters' faith formation rather than subverts it. The essential read for all patriot parents in America!"
— Jack Posobiec, *New York Times* Bestselling Author, *Human Events* Senior Editor, and Veteran Navy Intelligence Officer

"This book arrives at a pivotal moment. My friend, Dr. Kent Ingle, rightly reminds us that our nation—and our universities—stand at a civilizational crossroads. Our future is not fixed; Christianity's influence is not assured—but neither is its decline inevitable. This is a defining time for God's people to contend for the Gospel across every profession and walk of life. *College Without Communism* offers a clear and hopeful vision for raising up a new generation of leaders—anchored in truth, marked by excellence, and emboldened with courage—who abide deeply in Christ and are prepared to meet this moment."
—Kristen Waggoner, President, Alliance Defending Freedom

"*College Without Communism* is a timely call for Christian conservatives to re-engage in higher education. Our universities shape the leaders of tomorrow, and if we withdraw, we leave a vacuum that will be filled by voices hostile to faith, family, and freedom. This book reminds us that our presence on campus is essential to defend truth—and to enrich the academic world with wisdom, dignity, and hope. A powerful read for anyone who believes higher education should be a marketplace of ideas, not an echo chamber."
— Dr. Jeremy Johnson, President, Northwest University

"As pastors, we've seen firsthand how culture pulls young people away from truth. *College Without Communism* is a powerful reminder that Christian higher education can still shape disciples who change the world, not just survive it."

— Tommy Barnett, Pastor, Dream City Church

"For too long, Christians have stepped back from higher education, and the consequences for our culture have been severe. In *College Without Communism*, Dr. Ingle issues a timely challenge to re-engage and see higher education campuses as mission fields. With clarity and conviction, he calls us to reclaim education and restore the foundations of truth so the next generation can flourish."

— Luke Barnett, Pastor, Dream City Church

"College campuses were once crucibles by which students were taught critical thinking skills, which then allowed them to apply those skills to an array of diverse thoughts, theories, and ideologies to learn how to arrive at the truth. Many colleges and universities today have significantly strayed from this course, choosing instead to accommodate the feelings of the students and hide from them anything that may be deemed offensive, thus denying the students the opportunity to truly understand and appreciate America's greatness and its struggles. In his book, Dr. Ingle and Mr. Lisec expose how the liberal Left, through 'woke' ideologies, are denying students the fulfillment of truly being able to reach their greatest potential. Progressive tactics are preventing students from being able to independently think for themselves and thereby denying them the necessary skills to objectively arrive at the truth. This is must-reading for any conservative parent."

— Dennis Ross, Former U.S. Congressman, Founder of the American Center for Public Leadership

"*College Without Communism* is a thought-provoking read for anyone interested in learning more about the shifting landscape of higher education in the United States. Kent and Joshua expose the perils of mission drift and ideological shifts, offering practical advice for future students and parents. This book is an invaluable guide for Christian families seeking to navigate higher education without compromising Biblical orthodoxy and orthopraxy."

— Philip E. Dearborn, President, Association for Biblical Higher Education

For Charlie Kirk—he fought the good fight and received his eternal reward. Now, it's your turn to do the same.

"Would a guy like JD Vance have been better off for America if instead of going to Yale he became a plumber?"
— @PatTheSecond, X

Authors' Note

While this book is co-authored by both Dr. Kent Ingle and Joshua Lisec, all anecdotes and insights after Joshua's foreword are relayed from the perspective of Dr. Ingle and from his role as President of Southeastern University. Expect the first-person pronouns *I*, *me*, *mine*, and so forth, with the exception being the foreword written from Joshua's first-person view. Thank you for your attention to this matter.

CONTENTS

Foreword by Joshua Lisec i

PREFACE: Win Our Schools, Win the Culture v

INTRODUCTION: Conservatives Have a College Problem ix

CHAPTER 1:
The Ancient Case for College 1

CHAPTER 2:
Late-Stage Education and the Decline and Fall of the Elite University 13

CHAPTER 3:
What Happens When Conservative Students Get a Liberal Education 27

CHAPTER 4:
How the College-to-Career Pipeline Broke 35

CHAPTER 5:
How Universities Can Do Better 43

CHAPTER 6:
How to Prepare for College Long Before College 53

CHAPTER 7:
Getting Everything We Can out of the College Experience 61

CHAPTER 8:
How to Finish School Strong and Get a Best First Real Job 71

CHAPTER 9:
Going Back to College for the Very First Time 77

CHAPTER 10:
The Truth about the Trades, Associate's Degrees, and
Professional Certifications 87

CHAPTER 11:
AI and the Future of Education 97

CHAPTER 12:
A Special Message: How College-Educated Homemakers &
Stay-at-Home Moms Will Save Western Civilization 107

APPENDIX: For the Christian Student at a Secular College 115

Acknowledgments 119
About the Authors 121
Endnotes 123

Foreword by Joshua Lisec

Communism is everywhere. Look anywhere. In government, despite recent conservative electoral victories. Still in the media. All over the arts and in entertainment. Big business and small alike. The family. Even religion. And, of course, in education.

This is the premise of my 2024 book *Unhumans: The Secret History of Communist Revolutions (And How to Crush Them)*, co-authored with independent journalist and veteran U.S. Navy intelligence officer Jack Posobiec. Endorsed by now-Vice President JD Vance, the *Unhumans* book presents a terrifying hypothesis that tens of thousands of readers believe to be true—that we, the people of the United States of America, have been enduring a slow-walked, multi-generational, right-under-our-noses far-Leftwing takeover of all American institutions, public and private.

The word *unhuman* is, of course, a verb. It means to deprive a person of the sacred rights to life, liberty, and property . . . starting in reverse order. This has been the playbook of every Left-wing political and social revolution of the last quarter-millennia. "This is what they do. Every single time," Jack and I write.

And it's this anti-Christian, anti-human ideology—this "woke mind virus" first conjured in the mad-science labs that were the minds of history's malcontents and miscreants—that is now the prevailing worldview of secular academia. As we write in *Unhumans*, Chapter 9: New American Founding, the infiltration and subversion of universities took place gradually, then all at once, during a single devastating, degenerate decade:

> Consider the conjunction of influences in 1960s America in the same geographic locations. The campus explains it all . . .
>
> Left-leaning individuals were already inclined to enter academia, and the hiring environment in those days was hospitable to PhDs who sought tenure. Furthermore, universities in that time tended to let go of professors who were too old, so many old positions were opened up. This allowed radicals to swarm the academy at all levels, leading to an academic culture that was and is left-wing through and through. In many university departments today, more than 90 percent of all

faculty are not just liberal but identify with far-left views. The roots of today's campus radicalism lie in the 60s because that era's radicals were in the right place at the right time.[1]

We've been struggling with the communistic indoctrination of every subsequent generation of students ever since. Now, some might take issue with this explicit use of the word *communism*. *After all*, reasons the righteous American patriot, *President Ronald Reagan defeated the Soviet Union. Soviet communism is over; long live freedom!*

Yes, yes, very good. But as Dr. Kent Ingle will reveal to you in *College Without Communism*, Left-wing radicalism mutated once outside the Iron Curtain. We've all seen the documentaries and browsed the history textbooks featuring brutal (and brutalist) totalitarian dictatorships of the Soviets, the Chinese Communist Party, Castro's Cubans, the Khmer Rouge, and more. But here in the West, all the while, the initial socioeconomic focus of Karl Marx has zoomed out—from a critique of capitalism to condemnation of *any* "have" over those who "have not." Some call this new Cultural Marxism "wokeness"; others, "gay race communism," with its elevation of homosexuality over traditional marriage, its quasi-worship of anyone non-white (who also happens to be a Leftist), and the elimination of mutual respect between men and women. "This is what they do. Every single time."

And all this, as Dr. Ingle will show, is the prevailing lens through which all reality is curated—and taught—on the modern American campus. Thus, each generation of religious leader, social worker, educator, business leader, government employee, media professional, and artist and entertainer has been . . . what?

What have they been?

Indoctrinated.

Exactly.

How often?

Every single time.

Higher education is the nerve center of the mutated Cultural Marxist organism. And unfortunately, the conservative move away from higher education has allowed this to happen virtually unchallenged. It's become a trope of conservative and even Christian guidance counseling to not "waste time getting a four-year degree" but rather to "become a plumber" or otherwise "enter the trades."

Let me ask you something.

How many U.S. Supreme Court Justices are certified in HVAC? And what percentage of Fortune 500 Chief Executive Officers have a college degree? How about this one... Which Hollywood A-list actors and actresses skipped school and went self-taught? The answers are *none, almost 100 percent*, and *so few that they're the exception and not the norm*.

I myself have attended three colleges, have two degrees, and two certifications (a master's-level and a professional) acquirable only through school.

"But look at all the billionaires who were dropouts!" some would fuss. And now we're back to the exceptions-not-the-norm rule. We've also sleight-of-handed ourselves into a different topic. Are we arguing for blue- and gray-collar workforce participation, or for refusal to participate in the radically anti-conservative schooling of our young people during the most impressionable period of adulthood—the late teens and early twenties?

Without irony and not as a joke, Dr. Ingle's book will make the best case for the trades you've probably ever read. At times, you might confuse him for Mike Rowe. That's OK. And on another note, the conservative Christian student can be *in* the world but not *of* the world. In fact, you don't even have to be "in" the "world" to earn college degrees!

Consider Southeastern University (SEU). Unlike some conservative Christian colleges, Southeastern—where Dr. Ingle serves as president—walks the talk. SEU is strategically positioned to be a bastion of truth and conservative values while fighting back on a national scale against the ideology of most major institutions. Here, Christian students are formed. Guided. Shaped. Mentored. And launched—into successful careers, vocations, and ministries, from chief executive officer to chief executive of the home. Yes, Southeastern is a rare institution that valorizes Proverbs 31 motherhood. This is a good and safe campus to send daughters and sons alike; I have both. I have authored this Foreword not just as Dr. Ingle's writing partner on *College Without Communism*, but as a fellow father. He gets it.

I also want communism out of schools, specifically its current rendition of dehumanization, Cultural Marxism. All human beings have dignity in the eyes of God; any ideology that says otherwise has none in ours.

Kent is a good man, a good father, and a good author, as you will soon see for yourself. And, of course, a good walker-of-the-talk. Earlier in his career, he witnessed anti-Christian teachings seep into one institution after another. Until he couldn't take it anymore. Enter, Southeastern. This is a haven in Florida where faculty who know better than to teach the wickedness of woke are free to teach truth—and students are free to learn it, share it, study it, and run with it.

More than anything, *College Without Communism* is an alternative to the degenerate postmodern campus—I mean, indoctrination factory. And even if you, your student, or your child or grandchild does have to endure a season on such a campus, this book will be a godsend. This book will equip you or your loved one with the truth, prepare you to make the most of college, enter the workforce with an upper hand, and survive and thrive it all with your faith intact.

This is the essential read for Christian parents, grandparents, students, professors, administrators, career counselors, youth pastors, and for anyone else who wants to reclaim the American college campus for Christ, starting with your student's walk with Him.

Welcome to *College Without Communism*.

Joshua Lisec

3x Father, 2x *New York Times* Bestselling Author, Author of *Unhumans: The Secret History of Communist Revolutions (And How to Crush Them)* with Jack Posobiec
Follow on X at @JoshuaLisec

Preface: Win Our Schools, Win the Culture

President Ronald Reagan, one of my political heroes, had a quote he always used to say: "Freedom is never more than one generation from extinction."

It sounds hyperbolic or alarmist, but it rings true, especially today. Some may say it's an overreaction; I sympathize, because it is a horrifying thought. Nobody *wants* to believe it. But we saw that very quote play out firsthand during the presidential election in the fall of 2024. Our nation stood at a crossroads between freedom and oppression, and thank God we chose freedom.

We need to invest in the next generation. Especially education. Not just so our kids can grow up to get degrees and have successful careers, but so they can learn how to think, vote, and engage civilly with society, so that the next generation, and the next, and the next, hold strong in the cause of freedom.

And it is under attack.

You couldn't have missed it. Histrionic shrieks of "banning books!" when parents ask to remove graphic sexual content from elementary and middle school libraries. Teachers going behind parents' backs to preach radical new social doctrines and convincing students to "transition" to the opposite sex.[1] Or going on unhinged rants about President Donald J. Trump at the sight of a student wearing a *Make America Great Again* hat.[2]

Our children's minds are under assault. They are targeted by an ideology, a philosophy, and a worldview that wants them to think that truth is relative. Regarding American history, they present their party line as "accurate." They are urged to reject the values that their parents taught them and that our country was built upon as the trickery of oppressors. Our children are being indoctrinated by a philosophy that wants them confused, lonely, and isolated.

This is the worldview of the Left—the philosophy of "Woke." It's not just an ideology, it's an ideology with a mandate to *conquer*. Our schools? Colonies where their agendas are pushed as fact. Our children's minds? Mere clay to mold as they see fit.

And while things have changed—both in my home state of Florida and in the capital of the country—it's still an uphill battle in enemy territory. An exaggeration? Hardly. From elementary school up to colleges and universities, the Left has been using school systems to attack our values, undermine our religions, and indoctrinate our children for decades.

They've been aided and abetted by bureaucratic bloat. Since the founding of the Department of Education in 1979, under President Jimmy Carter, costs, regulations, and mandates have gone *up* for schools, while test scores and academic achievement have gone *down*. The more money the government pumps in (accompanied, of course, by "helpful" requirements and guidance), the worse students perform.

This is what we're up against.

Here's the hard truth: You can raise your children and grandchildren to love God, love this country, and know right from wrong—but if you send them off to a woke educational institution, everything you've instilled in them is at risk. We've all seen the headlines. The antisemitism. The hatred. The chaos. We've watched as these once-prestigious educational institutions have not only tolerated violence and division but have openly defied law and order.

You know their names. These schools, once shining examples of academic excellence, have devolved into ideological battlegrounds—hostile to faith, hostile to truth, and hostile to the very values that built this nation.

But there's change in the air. For too long, we have sat complacent, doing nothing, entrusting our children to ideologues who want to make them *their* children. States are starting to take notice. They're starting to join the fight.

I already have. I've had the privilege of serving as the president of Southeastern University for fifteen years as of this writing. We have our traditional campus in Lakeland, Florida, and boast network campuses nationwide. We're a faith-based university, offering an environment rich with meaning and purpose.

Our enrollment shows as much. We've had twelve straight years of record enrollment, going from about 2,400 students when I first became president to nearly 12,000 in 2024. In fact, *The Chronicle of Higher Education* named us the second-fastest growing private, non-profit, doctoral-level institution in the nation, and our enrollment has soared by 362 percent since 2011. Our academic programs are designed to get our students an education without burying them alive in debt.

We're faith-based, but we're also offering more than 115 degree programs, from associate's degrees to doctorates. We've gone from nine to twenty different sports programs. And, if I may say so myself, pretty successful sports programs. We've won 78 Sun Conference Championships and 17 NAIA

National Championships. And we did so without letting biological males invade women's sports, even with pressure from the previous presidential administration of Joe Biden.

"But wait!" our critics might say, "aren't you just the mirror image of what you're complaining about? Aren't you just indoctrinating on the other side?"

We're not afraid of our faith. The Founding Fathers of the United States of America recognized the importance of integrating religious belief into our nation's values. Almost every national monument in Washington, D.C., quotes Scripture. For them, faith is the bedrock, the wellspring from which all of their beliefs flowed.

The ones trying to excise that faith—the beliefs that protected our freedoms, even the freedom to disagree—are the ones breaking with the past and waging a war on their own history.

President Reagan warned us about freedom going extinct. He also said, elsewhere, "Our leaders must remember that education doesn't begin with some isolated bureaucrat in Washington. It doesn't even begin with state or local officials. Education begins at home, where it is a parental right and responsibility."

We're not the ones fighting the parents, hiding what we're teaching from them. We're the ones working with parents and students to instill faith and civic responsibility into our students. We're preparing them to engage with the world, rather than convert them to mentally narrowed activists who are trying to change the world in a desperate attempt to soothe the emotional abuse their professors had instilled within them.

And on that note, I can go no further without mentioning Charlie Kirk. I had a private meeting with Charlie and my colleague Dr. Michael Steiner on SEU's campus in 2022. We instantly knew we were on the same mission. Unfortunately, we never got the opportunity to execute on the dreams we discussed that day. Even from that brief time together, we were forever changed men. Charlie called us to think differently and more deeply about our roles as leaders in higher education. It has always been my conviction to build the kind of university that Charlie longed for—one where an open and honest dialogue of ideas could help students form their faith and launch out into the bright futures God has planned for them.

The future of our nation always has been—and always will be—shaped on the college campus. It was an honor and a privilege to witness Charlie's influence on campuses. His life's work marked a turning point for our country.

Charlie created a moment to restore what was lost and to create a new vision for the future of academia—and for America. It's now up to us to make sure that moment becomes a movement. May this book serve that endeavor.

I am proud to be serving the parents and students of Southeastern University and raising the next generation to fight for freedom. And in these next pages, I hope to show you how to join me in that fight—to take back academia, and make higher education great again!

Introduction: Conservatives Have a College Problem

What do conservatives at large think of higher education? I'll be honest . . . it's not looking good. Take this headline from the Manhattan Institute, a conservative think-tank: "Why Conservatives Are Turning Against Higher Education."[1] The article itself talks about the attempts to divest the college degree of its status as the gateway to a prosperous life.

Or take a look at this line from a *USA Today* opinion piece: "Young conservatives like me are told not to attend college. That's shortsighted."[2] While I agree, yes, it's shortsighted, I also agree that so much conservative media pushes our young people away from higher education.

Follow that *USA Today* op-ed up with this gem from the James G. Martin Center for Academic Renewal: "The Plight of College Conservatives."[3] Ha! It almost sounds like a *National Geographic* special about some endangered species—the rare and elusive Christian student in a secular habitat. Other hot takes on the subject are more skeptical of this "plight," like this one from the AAUP with the headline, "Rethinking the Plight of Conservatives in Higher Education."[4] While the post pushes back against the idea that conservatives are discriminated against, it does seem to presume that the reader would themselves assume conservatives are persecuted on college campuses (whether or not that's actually true, being a separate matter).

And true it is. According to the Manhattan Institute, "We Have the Data to Prove It: Universities Are Hostile to Conservatives."[5] This particular article detailed how both "hard and soft authoritarianism are pervasive in academia."[6] Any student reading that—or any parent—is looking for a place to get an education, not come face to face with tyrannical authoritarianism that demands students of a certain race feel guilty for looking the way they do, or denying the biological reality that "male and female He created them."

That's probably why this particular article from the *Washington Examiner* exists: "How to avoid professors who penalize conservatives."[7] A handy guide to figuring out which professor will attack you over your personal beliefs. Priming you to reconsider going to college, thinking, *'Maybe it's not worth it if my teachers are going to be targeting me.'*

What do our adversaries on the Left think about this? Vox puts it succinctly: "Conservatives have long been at war with colleges."[8] It's a bad thing, of course, for Vox. That article portrayed fighting discriminatory DEI practices and affirmative action as a "crusade against higher education."[9]

Then there's this opinion piece from *The Seattle Times*, with a headline promising to reveal "Why conservatives fear higher education."[10] We aren't just disdainful of it, haven't you heard? We *fear* it. Apparently we live in terror at the thought of . . . well, *thought*. It's probably news to you. But even though I am president of an institute of higher learning, it's not news to me; I know why people think this about conservatives, and it's not just bigotry on their part.

Conservative media has long since focused on the liberal bias in higher education. Story upon story inundate our televisions or our phones, fill our social media feeds with tales of conservative students targeted by their liberal counterparts or hectored and mocked by their teachers. We see cases where the lone conservative faculty member gets singled out for discipline, just because that teacher doesn't align with the enforced consensus of the rest of the group. We hear about the bad grades students get for writing papers that don't mindlessly parrot liberal orthodoxy.

It's no wonder that pundits warn about sending your kid to a college that's likely to be hostile to their beliefs. Sometimes, they come back changed, almost possessed by a new ideology, often sporting fashion styles, piercings, and hair colorings that seem more ugly than rebellious, showcasing how radical the break with their past selves have been. But often, conservative freshmen enter their sophomore years not as newly-minted communists, but still as conservatives. Just demoralized. Beaten down. Afraid to actually discuss what they believe, out of fear that their teachers, or even their own classmates, would turn against them. Who in their right mind, these pundits say, *would* send your kid there?

If we lose our schools, we lose our culture. And some on our side have already given up. Now, I don't blame these people. They're doing what they think is best, protecting their children. But while it might be protective on a personal level, on the cultural stage, it's surrender. It's the total abandonment of any civic interaction. And it's robbing America of its potential.

Think about that tweet at the beginning of the book. **"Would JD Vance have better helped America if he had been a plumber? Would Thomas Sowell have done better for America if he hadn't gone to Harvard?"**

While it's all well and good to valorize those who pursue the trades, this shouldn't come at the cost of demonizing higher education. It's understandable *why* higher ed is a favored punching bag for conservative pundits, but the message is a shortsighted one.

Liberals are "out-degreeing" conservatives. Look at the statistics; according to the American Enterprise Institute, "60 percent of the faculty identified as either far Left or liberal compared to just 12 percent being conservative or far Right" in 2016 to 2017.[11] Look back a few decades, in 1989, and the ratio of liberal to conservative was 2.3 to 1, drifting up to 5 to 1 in 2016.[12]

The American Enterprise Institute notes that this wasn't because the country shifted left; in fact, the country had a normal distribution (sometimes called a bell curve distribution) with most of the country remaining moderate, with approximately equal amounts of people identifying as conservative or liberal.[13] The country remained that way, and didn't shift to a five-to-one ratio of liberal to conservative, and in fact, has a general trend towards centrism.[14]

College education is a factor in voting patterns. While decades ago, it didn't seem to matter that much. In 2016, the majority of college-educated voters swung Democrat. In the 2024 election, college-educated men were evenly split between Democrat Kamala Harris and Trump, while college-educated women swung 61 percent towards then-Vice President Harris.[15]

Why is this important? After all, aren't we trying to push more people towards trades? And aren't giant companies like IBM and Google removing the requirements to have a college degree?

Forget that even today, with colleges actively working to devalue the goodwill they've been entrusted with for generations, degrees still confer prestige and status in terms of hiring; most entry level jobs still require them. And while some conservatives will try to fight that, in the meantime, if they don't let their own children attain a college degree, they're setting their kids up to struggle in the current world we live in.

Colleges offer internships as well. These can be springboards into gainful employment for the students beyond merely offering hands-on experience. They also offer credentialing, needed for things like medicine, or becoming a CPA.

Bemoan it all you want, this is the world we live in. As conservatives, we're realists; we deal with the facts on the ground, as they are. Our philosophical roots go back to Aristotle, Augustine, Burke, Locke, and the Founding Fathers. It is the Left that lives in the world they would prefer exists. But right now, we're giving all of the opportunities for advancement to the Left.

A degree is a key that unlocks institutions. If you want to get into medicine, law, politics, or civil service, you *need* a college education.

Let's do a thought experiment. Let's imagine that the majority of conservative parents have woken up to the fact that their local elementary, middle, and high schools have been colonized by the Left. College, too, has been similarly occupied.

Let's say these parents have been lucky. Their kids have gotten their high school diplomas, and by the grace of God have *not* been brainwashed into being anxious communists. These parents are breathing a sigh of relief. It was touch and go for a while, after all. But then, after high school, they need to help their children find the right path through life.

On the one hand, they could risk it, roll the dice, and go into debt to see their child sent to yet another indoctrination center. Honestly, that they have to saddle their kid with debt is just a kick in the teeth. But just down the road, not ten minutes away, is a trade school. Sure, it's not as glamorous, the conservative parents think. But it's honest work, and *not* co-opted by Leftists. And significantly cheaper! The answer is obvious. But the outcome?

Consider liberal parents. They're not worried about indoctrination; what the schools preach, they believe. Maybe not *everything;* the parents are kind of confused on the whole "gender is a spectrum" thing, but the people behind it have their hearts in the right place, obviously. There's no *risk* in their minds in sending their children to college.

(Of course, some of these parents are discovering that the Leftist beliefs their children adopt are incredibly intolerant of anyone who isn't *as* radical as they are, and are finding themselves bewildered when their own kids cut them off for not being extreme enough!)

What happens? Fewer conservatives enter higher education, and proportionally more liberals leave with college degrees. Academia recruits more liberals, creating an environment even *more* closed off to conservatives. Which means that less conservatives enter higher education, and proportionally more liberals leave with college degrees. Which means academia recruits more liberals, creating an environment even *more* closed off to conservatives. Which means that less conservatives enter higher education, and proportionally more liberals leave with college degrees. Which means—

You get the picture. It's a vicious cycle, and one that casts ripples across all sectors of society. What happens when most lawyers are not only trained by Leftists, but are themselves of the Left? You get lawfare against conservative and Christian causes. What happens when doctors are steeped in Leftist ideology? You get the madness that is "gender-affirming care," where doctors mutilate perfectly healthy children in the name of some made-up "gender identity." What happens when most business analysts and advisors are schooled by Leftists? You get more corporate-mandated DEI programs and ESG score obsessions. What happens when you hand the keys to the major institutions of society to the Left? You get where we are now, where it seems every corporation is hellbent on advancing anti-Christian values and anti-American priorities. You get a culture whose leaders are hostile to its very existence.

This fight for the future is personal. In the mid-to-late 1990s, my wife and I made six trips to Romania to adopt our three children. This was just after the fall of the Nicolae Ceaușescu regime, when the country was still reeling from the devastations of communism. What I witnessed there will never leave me.

We walked into massive orphanages filled with hundreds of children. Parents had been forced to give them up simply because they could not afford to care for them. I saw babies laying in rows on the floor, abandoned in horrendous conditions; they were hungry, neglected, and without hope. These children weren't there because their parents didn't love them. They lay abandoned because a society built on communist ideology had destroyed families and stripped people of opportunity.

Those images are burned into my mind. I know what happens when a culture embraces an ideology that undermines family and faith. I have seen it. Heard it. Wept over it. My wife and I rescued three beautiful souls from it. And now, years later, I am terrified to see the same ideology infiltrating our nation, with academia being a primary distribution channel. That's also why I'm excited about this book—I wrote this to raise awareness of the danger we face and to call us all to action before it's too late.

But in a well-meaning yet misguided attempt to protect their own children, conservative Christians have been opting out of institutions such as higher education. Even Christian colleges. And in a sickening twist, this refusal to engage actually *helps* the Left. Conservatives are *getting out of their way.*

Some people think the answer is to burn down everything. Colleges and universities had a good run, they say, but the real answer is to let them die, and something else will replace them. Maybe it's online tutorial classes.

Maybe it's the gig economy. Maybe it's whatever buzzword they can think of.

But colleges were meant to be something else. The university was a Christian institution, founded to provide a godly education in medieval Europe, though its roots stretch back to the traditions of Athens. There's no reason that the current corruption of its form can't be reversed. There's no reason colleges can't recall what they were meant to be, and return to what they once were.

As Christians, we are called to be salt and light to the world. At Southeastern University, we've always prided ourselves on our civic engagement, and consider it a crucial part of a student's education. We have not given up on engaging with the world, and we want to prepare our students to help make it a better place.

And where do we start with that? Where anyone starts: at the beginning.

CHAPTER 1
THE ANCIENT CASE FOR COLLEGE

I DIDN'T GROW UP IMAGINING I'D ONE DAY BECOME THE president of a university. At eighteen, I wasn't headed off to an elite private college with a ten-year plan in hand; I was enrolling at my local community college while working as a rookie sports broadcaster for the NBC affiliate in Bakersfield, California. Back then, I only knew two things for sure: one, that I loved communicating, and two, that I wanted to help people. I just didn't know yet how those two passions would shape my future purpose.

Broadcasting became my first career, opening doors I never expected. But when I felt the call to ministry, I knew I couldn't lead without first learning, so I went back to school. But this time, it wasn't just to earn a degree. I had a grand purpose: to pursue the kind of knowledge that would empower me to better serve others. This would include church history, systematic theology, and organizational leadership. Every season of life brought new opportunities; I treated each as a chance to grow into the kind of leader God was shaping me to be.

Eventually, that path led me to a university deanship—and then, unexpectedly, to the presidency of Southeastern University. It still amazes me. But that's the power of education when it's more than earning credentials or climbing ladders. There is a true, chief purpose to education, and I realized that it's far more than degrees and careers; it's preparation for your life calling.

That said, something I learned in my own education is that to truly understand what a thing is for, what its grand purpose in life is, you must understand its function. What it does, what it was meant to do, what its design entails. The fancy word, used by philosophers since Aristotle, is *teleology*.

A *telos* is the Greek way of saying a *purpose* or a *chief end*. To say that this is the cornerstone of Western philosophical thought would be a gross understatement; it is how we think about the world. "But Dr. Ingle," you may say, "I'm no philosopher. I don't think about this teleology thing at all!"

That's not quite true. Sure, you may not sit in a dusty office or book-stuffed study and contemplate the nature of a thing's nature (with the appropriate "hmms" and "Eureka!s" to make sure anyone walking by the door knows you're involved in some Very Important Thinking), but you think *according* to teleology. Let me put it another way:

"The purpose of a thing is what it does."

"But Dr. Ingle," you might protest again, "that's common sense!" It is now, and that's all thanks to our intellectual ancestors.

Everyone uses teleology; it is not just the domain of the philosophy grad student with his or her head in the clouds (and nowadays, secular philosophy grads are more likely to be studying Marxism or French existentialism or homicidal postcolonial theory instead of the rich tradition of Western Civilization's heritage.) Engineers, doctors, veterinarians, plumbers, architects . . . Everyone thinks according to the chief ends of things; it's the invisible, oftentimes unthought-about scaffolding upon which all of our intellectual development rests.

Take engineering. If someone is designing a jet engine, each component of that engine has a *telos* that *must* be fulfilled, or else the engine fails to work (whether that's just not turning on or exploding). A part's *telos* could be as complex as "injects fuel into another part of the engine" or as simple as "holds these other parts together, even under a lot of force." If any of those parts don't fulfill their chief end (the fuel injector doesn't inject fuel, the bracket holding the entire engine together snaps, etc.) then you don't have a working engine.

Or consider biology. What is the purpose of an animal's paw? It's to facilitate walking and to bear the weight (or at least part of the weight) of the creature it belongs to, whether that's a majestic grey wolf, a tiger, your neighbor's annoying housecat, or your adorable golden retriever named Rover. But if one day you see Rover limping around to avoid using one of his paws, you know something has gone wrong, and you rush him to the vet.

It's even part of Western religious tradition. In the Catholic faith, St. Thomas Aquinas spent his life marrying the teleological thought of Aristotle to the beliefs of Christians. But this is not just on one side of the Reformation. The Westminster Shorter Catechism, with its question and answer format designed to induct new members into the faith, opened with this question: "What is the chief end of man?" The answer? "Man's chief end is to glorify God, and to enjoy him forever."[1]

So important is teleology to our way of life that our faiths put it first, and all of our sciences depend on it for their function.

Then what is the function of **college**? What is its purpose? What is its teleology? And more crucially, where, how, and when has it gone away from that?

The Beginning of Academia: Plato, the Academy, and the Socratic Method

When you first crack open one of Plato's books of philosophy, you're often surprised. You don't know what you're expecting; maybe paragraphs upon paragraphs of technical jargon to "prove" obscure points of archaic philosophy about as clear as mud (that's more Aristotle). Or maybe you were expecting a lot of technical equations, as if it was a kind of mathematics.

What you get instead, is dialogue.

Pick up the *Symposium* (about the nature of love), or his *Republic* (about statecraft), or any of the other "dialogues" like the *Euthyphro* or *Critias,* and what you get isn't a long-winded lecture in prose form festooned with too many footnotes. What you get is what reads like a stage-play. Plato himself is oddly absent, but it is Socrates who takes center stage. Socrates, famous for knowing that he knows nothing (as opposed to the sages and priests and sophists of his time who knew nothing, but didn't realize they knew nothing), asking questions of his other interlocutors.

The genius of Socrates is revealed in these questions. He prods for a definition; then, finding one, he attacks it *mercilessly*, to see if it can stand up to scrutiny. Very often, the wise men that he is speaking to end up reeling; his questions often find little bits of their elegant philosophies that they had never considered. And those little exceptions that the sophists haven't considered? They usually end up being fatal to their worldview.

It was one of Socrates' other beliefs that prompted this, that the unexamined life was not worth living.

We get the Socratic Method from this rich tradition. This is a more unconventional teaching method wherein the teacher acts not as an unquestionable authority, nor even as a sidelined figure there to "help" the students learn on their own, but in almost an adversarial position, asking pointed questions designed to make the students think and consider not just what they believe, but why they believe it. The goal is to expose and examine the moral and ideological underpinnings of beliefs. It can be challenging; after all, it isn't pleasant to find out that the bedrock system of belief that you have relied on for years—that you have forged part of your identity on—is so flawed as to be untenable.[2]

But when they come out of it, the students have a deep insight into their beliefs, into all of the contingent beliefs that support them. They know the foundation, and the ground that their foundation is built upon, and the layers beneath that.

None of the dialogues of Socrates start with foregone conclusions that are then proven; the dialogues are acts of discovery, of archaeology. Thus Plato's philosophy—for it is Plato who presents these dialogues to us—are exploratory.[3] He doesn't set out, like so many woke professors today, with the goal of impressing a belief system on a person. Instead, the dialogues show men figuring out, piece by piece, what beliefs entail, and thus what it means to be good, or pious, or beautiful.

Plato founded his Academy, the first sort of university in ancient Europe, to try to fix the problems of his day and age. Socrates had been executed when the leading elite of Athens decided that his method of questioning and challenging presuppositions was too subversive, and before then, Plato had survived the reign of Athens' infamous Thirty Tyrants. They didn't even last a whole year but had managed to sow enough terror with their brutal dictatorship that Plato felt like he *had* to act.[4]

Leaders, he reasoned, could not get any better unless they learned what it meant to be *good*, or *just*. They needed a philosopher-king, a ruler schooled in philosophy.[5]

To this end, he set up the Academy. While it is often credited with being the first university (though that honor usually goes to the University in Bologna, which we'll stop by later), it didn't look like any of the modern college campuses we might think of, or even older ones like Oxford University in Britain (we'll get to that, too). It was something unique for the time.

Ancient Greece had a sort of elementary school program, for children primarily, to teach them how to read and write, how to do math, and how to build up other basic skills. Everything else, Athenian citizens were expected to pick up via cultural osmosis or by paying sophists to teach rhetoric. Now, sophists (where we get the word "sophistry," which is wordplay without any real relation to the truth) were not philosophers per se, but more like lawyers, able to make any argument *sound* persuasive, regardless of how true the argument is. As such, they were a frequent target of Socrates' pointed questions.[6]

Neither the childhood education system nor the polished but empty rhetoric of the sophists served Plato's goals of educating the future rulers of Athens, so he started the Academy, a *park*. There were no lecture halls, no towering offices; just a gymnasium for physical fitness, a sacred grove of olive trees, a house for private conversations and drinking parties (called *symposia*), and a handful of shrines and altars to several of the Greek gods, including, most fittingly, the Muses.[7]

Much of the public activity occurred in the campus or the gymnasium, where philosophers would discuss their ideas while walking the park or exercising. And while there were private events—conversations, parties, or other events hosted at the park—the genius of the thing was that it was surprisingly hands-off. Very few "classes" as we would know them were held; most of the intellectual activity was generated by the minds that flocked to the park and gymnasium.[8]

Like in his dialogues, Plato is oddly absent from his own school; he is recorded as having given only one lecture, "On the Good," which was mostly about mathematics, much to the surprise and confusion of all but his most devoted students. This was an institution where Socratic questioning was baked into the bricks, after all. And when it did step away from dialogues about ethics and deeper into the scientific research of mathematics, Plato didn't directly control anything; instead, he offered mathematical problems he thought the brilliant minds there ought to focus on. He issued challenges but didn't provide ready-made ideological solutions out of the box.[9]

Questions had gotten Socrates in trouble with the Athenian elite, who had forced him to drink poison. But questions had formed the bedrock of Plato's Academy—and shaped the path the Western mind would take forever after.

How to Think, Not What to Think: Aristotle, Alexander, and the Lyceum

When you crack open a tome of Plato's, you're greeted with lively dialogue. The characters spring to life, even if they are mere vessels for different belief systems.

Aristotle is different. He's meticulous, slowly pinning down every branching path an argument could make in painstaking detail. He's exhaustive; when he provides you a list, you can be sure that he double-checked it. And when he wrote down an argument, he made sure everything followed logically, in every way possible. In all honesty, he's kind of dull to read.

Aristotle was one of the students at Plato's Academy, studying under Plato himself, but he hailed from Macedonia. After his studies, however, he traveled around Asia Minor, settled down with a wife, and studied marine biology—until he got a request from King Philip of Macedon. The king had heard of Aristotle, you see, and wanted him to tutor his son before the prince would go off to military service.[10]

That prince's name? Alexander the Great.

Historians aren't quite sure how long that arrangement lasted, but while Alexander went on to start conquering the world, Aristotle eventually returned to Athens. This time, he created the Lyceum, a school out of a temple to Apollo. Like Plato's Academy, it was centered around a gymnasium, and physical exercise was a crucial part of the entire endeavor (Aristotle's preferred flavor was lots of walking around).[11]

Aristotle differed from Plato in one very important area. Where Plato was more concerned with the Forms, or these unchanging ideas of things like truth, beauty, goodness, etc.,[12] Aristotle was much more of a realist.[13] He often relied on credible opinions and observation rather than ruthless dialogue.[14]

Observation, experimentation, built on the work of those before them. This is the foundation for modern science. And while it would take Christian philosophy much later to truly perfect science, this was the first step towards that great tradition.

The Lyceum did something else incredibly crucial. Where Plato's Academy provided a haven for scholars to gather and debate, Aristotle's Lyceum became a repository for books and scrolls. Aristotle made it a point to systematically collect these texts to preserve them; the Lyceum became the first library in Europe.[15]

While the Academy was all about dialogue and interrogating, the Lyceum was about research and preservation. And when you look at the two ostensible purposes of the modern day university, what are they?

Teaching and research.

Aristotle didn't merely teach the man who would conquer most of the known world; he paved the way for the first libraries and introduced the realist tradition into our civilizational train of thought.

But how did we go from temples and gyms where smart people talked while they exercised to the university we know today, with classrooms and curricula and professors and the modern version of the ancient gymnasium—college sports?

It's time to go medieval on you.

No Separation of Church and College: The Middle Ages and the Seven Liberal Arts

Already, you can see some of the ancient roots of our university systems in Plato and Aristotle's time. The heart of it is there—finding a wise man to instruct students then paying them a fair wage to do so. But what helped us jump from walks among the trees of the Academy to the college campus we have today, with not one solitary sagelike figure, but a roster of purported experts in the field? This would be the medieval university.

Most education in the Middle Ages happened within churches and monasteries. In medieval times, education was linked to place and community. It wasn't a place that took away your kids and scrambled their brains, but a place where the community preserved and transmitted what it considered to be sacred to the next generation. Without the monasteries, we wouldn't even know who Plato, Socrates, and Aristotle were after the fall of Rome. This conservatism—the preservation of that which is essential to human flourishing—is also one of the foundational principles of *all* universities. So, as you can imagine, religious academia involved more than instruction on the priesthood and other faith-based life; European education of that day and age also included readings on philosophy and astronomy (as astronomy was both viewed as a way to plumb the depths of God's creation, as well as the more practical matter of telling time reliably, both for the various prayer times for the monastic orders and for more practical reasons like when to plant which crops.)[16]

But eventually, demand for education began to grow, and the monasteries could not keep up. While no doubt taking a look back to Plato and Aristotle as an inspiration, enterprising individuals also looked around them to the burgeoning private sector and to the organizations that dominated trades at the time: the medieval guild. Thus, masters of rhetoric and philosophy and law and medicine began to gather together with students and formed unions known by the Latin term *universitas*.[17]

Exactly when these *universitates* originated is harder to pin down, as the term referred specifically to the union of masters and students, and not to any set properties or official organizations with charters or the like.[18] We should also note the Salerno School, one of the first medical schools in the history of the West, was founded out of a monastery in Salerno, Italy, where many Greek and Arabic manuscripts had been gathered.[19]

However, what we consider the first real university started in the Italian city of Bologna.[20] This wasn't an official declaration from on high, at least not at first, but was born from the actions of a few of the students; it was a private institution.[21] Bologna claims to have been started in A.D. 1088,[22] although officially, the students won legal protection in the form of a charter in 1158 from none other than the Holy Roman Emperor himself.[23]

Not surprisingly, Bologna was best known as a law school, and as other groups of students and teachers organized, they began to specialize. The *universitates* of Padua and Montpellier, for example, were known for their training in medicine, and Paris boasted one of the finest schools of theology in the land. The same went for a certain university of Oxford in England, but we'll return to that later, as Oxford became famous for a different corpus of subjects.[24]

Here, students studied the works of Aristotle. The works of the Philosopher, as he was known, were their textbooks. But not just Aristotle; they read all sorts of things, like *De Sphera,* by John of Sacrobosco, written around A.D. 1230. While modern authors and commentators like to discuss the Medieval period as the Dark Ages, where religious superstition ruled the world and priests taught that the earth was flat because the Bible said so (a myth we owe to authors like Washington Irving, and then later scholars like Andrew

Dickson White, who popularized the fiction of an eternal fight between science and religion), scholars were already calculating the circumference of the sphere of the globe and getting to within a few thousand miles of its true measurement. Any inaccuracies on their end were more easily explained by this being an exercise to show such things *could* be calculated.[25]

Life in these universities, oddly enough, resembles what our modern day students would go through. Most of the time was spent studying, though there were a few holidays. The universities did offer student accommodations, but these were fairly spartan and uncomfortable, much like modern college dormitories. Students nowadays can take comfort in the fact that they also continue a time-honored tradition of being dirt poor as well, thanks to the exorbitant price of the books they need to study (on the other hand, one might imagine that none of the medieval masters made you buy their personal textbooks; they weren't Aristotle.) And while we might have hoped that the students, awash in a much more religious culture, would have been better-behaved in the medieval era, unfortunately that was not the case. Students in the present day might not realize it while they're partying, but they're doing exactly what their predecessors did in the olden days: making a drunken, rowdy nuisance of themselves to their not-so-happy neighbors.[26] The more things change, the more they remain the same.

But one thing did change, and that was the curriculum. Let's return to the University of Oxford. While it was known for its theology, Oxford was also famous long ago for its initial course in what is known as the Seven Liberal Arts.[27]

"But wait, Dr. Ingle," you might say, "isn't this whole book about how to avoid liberal indoctrination on college campuses? Why are you talking about liberal arts programs? Aren't those how we got into this mess?"

Well, the story is more complicated than that, but even so, when I refer to the Seven Liberal Arts, I'm not referring to Feminist Underwater Basketweaving, Queer Panamanian Cinematography, or Postcolonial Interpretive Dance. The Seven Liberal Arts were seven specific subjects designed to provide a foundation for further learning, dating back to Roman times, called "liberal" to denote they were subjects fit for free (and only free) men to learn.[28]

These seven disciplines were divided into a group of three called the *trivium*, consisting of grammar, rhetoric, and logic (sometimes referred to as dialectic), and a group of four known as the *quadrivium*, consisting of arithmetic, music, geometry, and astronomy. While the last group seems rather arbitrary, these were all considered very mathematical subjects; remember that in the Middle Ages, they used astronomy for timekeeping.[29] As Sister Miriam Joseph, C.S.C., Ph.D., puts in her seminal text on the *trivium*:

> The trivium includes those aspects of the liberal arts that pertain to mind, and the quadrivium, those aspects of the liberal arts that pertain to matter. Logic, grammar, and rhetoric constitute the trivium; and arithmetic, music, geometry, and astronomy constitute the quadrivium. Logic is the art of thinking; grammar, the art of inventing symbols and combining them to express thought; and rhetoric, the art of communicating thought from one mind to another, the adaptation of language to circumstance. Arithmetic, the theory of number, and music, an application of the theory of number (the measurement of discrete quantities in motion), are the arts of discrete quantity or number. Geometry, the theory of space, and astronomy, an application of the theory of space, are the arts of continuous quantity or extension.[30]

She goes on to say that in the modern day, "as in centuries past, a mastery of the liberal arts is widely recognized as the best preparation for work in professional schools, such as those of medicine, law, engineering, or theology. Those who first perfect their own faculties through liberal education are thereby better prepared to serve others in a professional or other capacity."[31] Keep in mind, when Sister Miriam Joseph refers to a "liberal education" she is not referring to the godless abomination of propagandized leftism that passes for "education" in our secular universities today. She is referring to something designed to promote human flourishing, what Aristotle called *eudaimonia*. Today, we might call it *truth*—and the pursuit of it. Universities were meant to be the institution in society where we assert, defend, and otherwise fight for truth, from the Judeo-Christian perspective. That's why schools used to teach *how* to pursue truth.

Consider the listed arts of the *trivium*. Rhetoric is about speaking, grammar about writing, logic about thinking. (As an aside, Southeastern University has an exclusive partnership with Classical Conversations, one of the largest homeschool curriculum organizations in the world. I first learned about the *trivium* from SEU's partnership on dual enrollment with Classical Conversations. They do excellent work. Learn more about our special relationship at www.seu.edu/admission/classical-conversations-plus.) In any case, the *trivium* is fundamental to communicating the ideas in your head. But what happens when you are missing any of them?

If you are lacking in logic, you will come up with theories that are not only nonsensical but collapse upon any scrutiny, like the Socratic questioning mentioned above. If you're missing the ability to interrogate your ideas so that they can remain internally coherent, then you're not able to come up with anything coherent to say.

If you are lacking in grammar, then when you attempt to put your thoughts to paper, you will get an unreadable mess. While avant-garde English departments might praise creative writing assignments with "unique" approaches to grammar, most people find these things impossible to read. You will produce the gibberish that clogs up most social media.

If you are lacking in rhetoric, when you speak, you will not be able to communicate clearly. When you write, the sentences might be coherent, but the meaning behind them will wash over the reader. Without a firm grasp of understanding *how* to say a thing, you cannot truly say you can *say* a thing.

Colleges, especially art colleges, place a primacy on self-expression. That's what art, or writing, or public speaking, is about. What they fail to realize is that by not teaching *how* to express oneself, they render their students effectively mute.

Maybe you've read the incoherent screeds of a newly-minted journalist fresh out of college. Maybe you've walked a campus and seen a bizarre art installation, or worse, those self-indulgent and esoteric acts of public insanity known as *performance art*. These are the results of a culture that refuses to teach students *how* to think, *how* to speak. They demand, instead, to teach them *what* to speak, and get incoherent, but ideologically conforming, gibberish as the output. As computer science majors like to say, "Garbage in, garbage out."

Telos: The Purpose of a University Is What It Does

What, then, was the purpose of the university?

Socrates focused on endless questioning of one's own beliefs, to make sure they stood up to scrutiny; Plato created an Academy where one could do that. Aristotle taught the importance of studying the natural world, and created one of the first academic libraries in his Lyceum. The medieval universities, starting in Bologna and spreading across the face of Europe, taught the Seven Liberal Arts to their students.

What did these have in common? These were not top-down institutions, enforced by the state for the interests of the state. They grew from the bottom up, whether they were the genius of one man (Plato or Aristotle) or the collective union of teacher and student (any *universitas* in Europe).

And more importantly, their foundations were teaching *how* to think in the pursuit of ultimate truth: about ourselves, about our world, and about God. Was there a risk of heterodoxy? Sure! But the goal wasn't to create a group of people who believed all the same things; it was to equip the students with the tools needed to figure out *why* they believed what they believed, and what underlying assumptions provided the foundations of those beliefs.

Ultimately, these institutions were meant to illuminate the mind, and show *how* to think, rather than *what* to think. They offered a chance to come alongside the great minds of their age, take in their wisdom, and, more importantly, learn to emulate them. Character was crucial; these were crucibles in which students were made wise, and taught the ways to elevate their thoughts. The world was an open book to them. Nothing ranked higher than truth; here, we taught centuries' worth of students the noblest means of its pursuit.

So how did it go so wrong? Where did we lose the plot? To find out, we're leaping far into the future, past the Renaissance and the Reformation, into Prussia, a region of modern-day Germany, soon after that nation's defeat at the hands of Napoleon Bonaparte.

CHAPTER 2
LATE-STAGE EDUCATION AND THE DECLINE AND FALL OF THE ELITE UNIVERSITY

IT IS THE BEGINNING OF THE NINETEENTH CENTURY. PRUSSIA, a state in what is now Germany, is reeling from its defeat at the hands of the man who had crowned himself emperor, Napoleon Bonaparte. Prussian leaders are scratching their heads, wondering, trying to figure out the one question on everyone's minds: *What went wrong?*

Their conclusions went inward. Their soldiers, and the citizenry from which their soldiers came, were too individualistic, too independent.[1] If only they had listened to their betters, their elites, they wouldn't have screwed up the war! Simple as that. The problem, you see, wasn't bad leadership; no, it had to be the *citizens* who were wrong, defective, and otherwise incapable of besting the Napoleonic hordes on the battlefield.

So the Prussian elites began to reorganize their education to better make their citizens into servile pieces of the machinery of the state; no more freethinking individuals.[2] Never again. So they birthed what some in America would soon praise as an enlightened policy—but what was ultimately a tyrant's dream: the Prussian school system.[3]

Consider your average anti-school choice activist. Leftist, usually, often with no children of their own (but plenty of ideas about how to raise *your* children). Ask them why they are so against school choice, and you'll get a myriad of answers. Perhaps you'll get the reasonable-sounding concern that the *quality* of the education won't be good enough, that parents or private schools cannot give an adequate education. Maybe you get concerns about fairness; private schools might perform better than public schools and offer their students an unfair advantage in life and so must be squashed for the good of all. Maybe you get to a common anti-religious sentiment, where they worry you won't teach evolution or gay rights. "Homeschoolers are just indoctrinating their children to hate gay and trans people," they say. "There's no other reason!" But ultimately, they all boil down to one commonality: the assumption that only the state can properly educate your children.

They would happen to agree with the despotic King Frederick the Great, who saw education not as a way to help one further ennoble himself and embrace his humanity, but as the essential tool of the absolute state, of which he had an "enlightened" right to rule. Where you have anti-school choice advocates complaining about the inequity of private schools, King Frederick William III's minister, von Stein, began his work dismantling any private schools he could find, consolidating all education under the Minister of the Interior.[4]

What came next was utterly predictable. The state has to certify all teachers via an examination, of course, and one must subject students to more and more tests, including a graduation examination. And, obviously, all of this must be supervised and monitored by the state, which means one needs an extensive array of bureaucrats to see that through. The common man, obviously, cannot manage it.[5]

But what about parents who resisted? Well, any recalcitrant families would get punished of course by the force of the state with no exceptions (except maybe physical or extreme mental disability). Should a child be truant? Then fines, civil penalties, and even removal of the child from the care of the "unfit" parents so that the state could explicitly raise them.[6]

Why? We hardly need to ask why the Prussian monarchs would want to further solidify their power over an institution; all governments seem to want to subsume everything they can. But why did Prussia's leaders focus so much on using education in their idea of absolute despotism?[7]

A large part of it boiled down to how the Prussian monarchs viewed themselves. In their minds, they were not the stewards of a people, subject to their whims, but the "head" to the nation's "body." *They* ruled, *they* thought, and the people obeyed, much like your arms obey you when you command them to move.[8]

The Prussian rulers had expanded the military and hardened the discipline to iron cruelty before demanding compulsory military service for their subjects. They had also strengthened the Civil Service, which would later metastasize into the infamous German bureaucracy, the likes of which would be satirized by authors like Franz Kafka. And these rulers had an extremely heavy hand on business, restricting and regulating them into servitude to the state. But all of that needed people to run it, after all, and the Prussian monarchs decided that it would make their rule a lot easier if they could inculcate submission to the state as early as possible (which happened to be age seven).[9]

The purpose of education was not, then, to make the students be able to think for themselves, but rather to fit in as cogs in the machine of the Prussian state. Individual genius? Unique contribution to the nation? Such a thing was deemed not to exist; the only genius was that of the sovereign. It was his world, and everyone else was just taking up space in it, so they might as well get a job to support the Most Important Man in the World.[10]

Consider the previous chapter. What was the point of the Seven Liberal Arts? To teach you how to think, and to create a basis for knowledge that one could expand across in any direction. What was the point of the Socratic method? It was to get the student to think about their own biases and to examine their life. How did Socrates end up? He died drinking hemlock after being accused of being subversive to the state. That really makes you think.

So how did schools go woke? How did we go from critical thinking to critical theory? And how did Judeo-Christian ethics get replaced by secular, anti-Christian, moral relativism throughout the institution of higher education?

Well, it all came from the man who at first seemed to despise absolute power in the state and hated that it molded people—only to hate it because it wasn't *him* doing the molding. His ideas, once adopted, transformed, and distributed, would result in the forfeiting of the Christian foundations of the United States of America to communist thought.

The Beginning of the End of Elite Universities: "Everything That Exists Deserves to Perish"

Who else would it be but Karl Marx? It's unfortunate, really, that he was as influential as he ended up being. As Paul Johnson recounts in his book *Intellectuals,* "Karl Marx has had more impact on actual events, as well as on the minds of men and women, than any other intellectual in modern times."[11] Indeed, many of the figures in the brief and acerbic biographies that followed Marx in the book were his disciples in some way.[12]

While Marx never started out to attack the Prussian schooling system, the greater aims of his "philosophy" would end up serving a similar purpose. But much like how the character of the Prussian monarchs shaped how they viewed the purpose of education, the character of Marx would shape those who would come after him, and how they would shape the world in turn.

Karl Marx was a scholar who had said of himself, "I am a machine condemned to devour books."[13] However, as scholars went, he did not seem to care about the accuracy of his facts, misrepresenting and citing sources of dubious quality or ignoring advances in the working conditions he was ostensibly so concerned about.[14]

He also seemed allergic to any kind of field research. He often got into fights with more working class revolutionaries like Pierre-Joseph Proudhon or William Weitling to withering criticism for not being philosophical enough, and being more concerned with the real life conditions of workers rather than abstract theorizing. And while he had a lifelong connection with Friedrich Engels, who hailed from an industrialist family, he never decided to see factory conditions for himself.[15]

So what, then, was the allure of Marx's philosophy? Why had his vision attracted so many people, if his facts and scholarship are so deficient? Again, we turn to Johnson:

> But in a deeper sense, he was not really a scholar and not a scientist at all. He was not interested in finding the truth but in proclaiming it. There were three strands in Marx: the poet, the journalist and the moralist. Each was important. Together, and in combination with his enormous will, they made him a formidable writer and seer. But there was nothing scientific about him; indeed, in all that matters he was anti-scientific.[16]

Marx's allure was that of a storyteller, more akin to a fire-and-brimstone preacher than an impassive researcher. As such, while most conservatives will delve into the insanity of his economic positions—such as his most famous one, communism—we're more interested in the state of the *soul* of Karl Marx. What animates his imagination? What moves him to (in his mind) righteous indignation?

Much of his moral outrage centered around moneylenders and usury, which he associated with the Jewish people in numerous diatribes too hideously anti-Semitic to even reproduce in text (and for those Leftists who happened to pick up this book by mistake, he hated black people just as much, and wrote about them with language so foul we can't reprint it here.) Much of this can be traced back to his own irresponsibility with money. The Marxes were always short on cash and lived well above their means, and much of the correspondence Karl Marx penned was to friends or family to ask them to send more money. He had even written to his friend Engels, upon hearing that Engels' mistress had died, wherein he briefly expressed his condolences, and then got down to the business of demanding more money from him (he had done something similar to his own mother after his father had passed away.)[17] At the very least, the Prussian school system did its best to instill diligence in its subjects.

But what else motivated Karl Marx? Many a great poet found themselves inspired by figures of the past, whether they were real or imagined; Dante famously wrote himself to be guided through the Nine Circles of Hell by Virgil, the poet who penned the *Aeneid*, while Homer invoked the Muses in the openings of both his *Iliad* and *Odyssey*. Who, then, was Marx's muse? Well, we ought to think back to Dante, for his particular literary guiding star was of a decidedly more *infernal* bent. But first, let's see what this mystery figure inspired.

Marx's poetry, Johnson notes, had two main topics. One was his eventual wife, Jenny von Westphalen. The other, sadly, was the topic of destroying the world. Suicide pacts, deals with the devil, and general destruction fascinated him. In the cosmic battle with Heaven and Hell, Marx was fascinated by the brimstone vapors of the Devil.[18]

Take, as an example, these lines from his two "Wild Songs." The first, a poem entitled "The Fiddler" has such gems as "'Why do I fiddle? Or the wild waves roar?/That they might pound the rocky shore,/That eye be blinded, that bosom swell,/That Soul's cry carry down to Hell.'" Which is, of course, followed up immediately by another gem of a line. "'How so! I plunge, plunge without fail/My blood-black sabre into your soul./That art God neither wants nor wists,/It leaps to the brain from Hell's black mists.'"[19] The other Wild Song is about two lovers, one of whom has drunk poison; her lover remains at her side while she dies.[20]

Or take his attempt at a play, entitled *Oulanem,* named after the main character. In one of the many ranting soliloquies of the play, you get such lines as "Soon I shall clasp Eternity and howl/Humanity's giant curse into its ear./Eternity! It is eternal pain,/Death inconceivable, immeasurable!" Or "Bound in eternal fear, splintered and void,/Bound to the very marble block of Being,/Bound, bound forever, and forever bound! . . . And we, we Apes of a cold God,…" These are not the musings of the philosopher but the rantings of a tortured soul, despairing not of mere pain, but of existence itself.[21]

Now, one could argue that this is the character of Oulanem, not Karl Marx, but even so, he bears the title of the play. And given Marx's aspirations for the play (he wanted it to be his generation's *Faust*), this was hardly an isolated set of ideas he happened to dream up for a character.[22] But let us leave aside his own amateur writing. Who inspired him? Who was his muse? We turn to the play he wanted to supplant, Goethe's *Faust*.

For those unaware, *Faust* is about a Doctor Faust (or Faustus, depending on which version of the story you encounter) who, bored of all worldly knowledge, turns to the occult and makes a wager with a devil known as Mephistopheles (or Mephisto). That's the inciting scene, and the rest of the play is Faust dealing with the consequences of his action.

So then is there almost a hint of ironic self-awareness in Karl Marx? Did he recognize his own Faustian tendencies to ally with dark forces to his inevitable doom? Did he realize that grasping for far beyond what man ought to reach for leads only to despair and ruin? One might assume that . . . if Marx had identified with the aged doctor of the tale. Instead, he opted for the devil. Yes, the eventual woke ideology that's overtaken American universities—which is itself a cultural mutation of Marxist communism—descends directly from demonic influence. This could not be clearer.

"Everything that exists deserves to perish!" That was Marx's favorite quote, among many, from Mephistopheles. He knew many of the devil's speeches from Goethe's play.[23] Consider the passages from *Oulanem*, then. Note the protagonist crying out at the *offense* of existence itself. Everything that exists, indeed! Life itself, *being* itself, is a hideous crime in Marx's eyes.

It also puts into a new perspective Marx's demand for "ruthless criticism of all that exists."[24] The book of Genesis tells us that God, upon viewing the completed Creation, called everything *good*. Marx's worldview called everything *bad*—so bad it "deserves to perish." That is woke spirituality, both homicidal and suicidal.

Ultimately, due to Marx's own pathological obsession with money and capital—he co-authored *The Communist Manifesto*, after all—he never focused exclusively on culture or education outside their association with old-world aristocracy and privilege. That would change with his followers, and of them, three stand out to explain why our schools have gone mad.

Marx's Dark Disciples: Gramsci, Marcuse, Freire, and Cultural Communism in Schools

Perhaps you have heard the phrase "long march through the institutions." You have, in a roundabout way, Antonio Gramsci to thank for it (though the term may have originated with a student activist named Rudi Dutschke.)[25]

Antonio Gramsci was born in Sardinia, Italy, to an Albanian family, and suffered from poor health ever since he had contracted tuberculosis as an infant. He was arrested by the Italian Fascists and imprisoned. His prosecutor had let slip the real reason the Fascists were cracking down on him: political opposition to Gramsci's Marxism. "We must stop this brain from functioning for twenty years," they said.[26]

What Gramsci ended up producing were the "Prison Notebooks," an analysis of communist revolutions that succeeded and those that failed. He moved on from economic Marxism to focus instead on culture and social institutions.[27] He recognized that to actually affect any change, the "cultural means of production" needed to be under communist control, not just factories and the like.[28] These things—churches, media, and *universities*—produced culture, and previous Marxists have neglected them in favor of trying to agitate the working class into accepting a revolution they didn't actually want.[29] As Dr. Samuel Gregg writes:

> Gramsci thought that all these cultural institutions weren't neutral, but in fact were serving as a vast propaganda machine on behalf of capitalism. Until leftists came to dominate them, they would never

be able to convince enough people to support their revolution.

This part of his thesis was like manna from heaven for many left-wing Western intellectuals. Instead of joining a factory collective or making bombs in basements, a leftist professor could help free society from capitalist exploitation by penning essays in his office or teaching students. In this scenario, the revolutionary force shifts away from the proletariat toward middle-class intellectuals.[30]

These cultural institutions produced a *hegemony,* according to Gramsci, that permitted some ideas while suppressing others. States had to cultivate consent, nowadays, which meant that they enforced a culture that prevented such revolutions.[31] Universities, as mentioned, were a part of this hegemony-generating process and thus must be captured from within. And as we know, higher education is itself a derivative of Christian civilization; without Jesus Christ, what we know as "college" would likely never have existed. Universities were meant to be the place of truth—about the natural world, the human social world, the spiritual world, and more. But if those universities could be infiltrated by everything-must-perish, anti-Christian ideas . . .

A contemporary of Antonio Gramsci was Herbert Marcuse, who we turn to next. Like Gramsci, Marcuse recognized that it would not be the workers of the world uniting due to economic conditions, but underclasses united by **culture**. Herbert Marcuse was part of a group of Marxist philosophers desperate to try to solve the "crisis of Marxism," which is a fancy way of saying that a number of Marx's predictions ended up not merely being false but flat out wrong. This group, the Institute for Social Research in Frankfurt, Germany, became known as the Frankfurt School, which fled the Nazis in the 1930s to settle in America. While most of the other Marxists returned to Germany, Marcuse settled in America permanently.[32] Lucky us.

Marcuse was often called the "guru of the student movement," with that movement being the chaotic protests of the 1960s. That said, he rejected this title, stating that it was he who had a lot to learn from students protesting the US military, capitalism, traditional marriage and family, and, of course, Christian morality and practice. In fact, Marcuse viewed student revolters as a revolutionary force, replacing Marx's beloved proletariat.[33] In fact, here's what he has to say about the idea of an old revolution against "technocracy," in his *Essay on Liberation*:

Such a revolution is not on the agenda. In the domain of corporate capitalism, the two historical factors of transformation, the subjective and objective, do not coincide: they are prevalent in different and even antagonistic groups. The objective factor, i.e., the human base of the process of production which reproduces the established society, exists in the industrial working class, the human source and reservoir of exploitation; the subjective factor, i.e., the political consciousness exists among the nonconformist young intelligentsia; and the vital need for change is the very life of the ghetto population; and of the "underprivileged" sections of the laboring classes in backward capitalist countries.[34]

In short, Marcuse explains, in painful academic jargon, that while you can have those *physically* "exploited" under capitalism exist as the workers, they don't *recognize* their "exploitation." The ones who can actually recognize it are often groups opposed to them: the "nonconformist young intelligentsia" he mentions. In other words, impressionable college students. Evil always targets the vulnerable.

Now, it wasn't just economic "exploitation" that Marcuse was worried about but a number of other forms of cultural domination. Sexual repression, for example, was a frequent concern of his (and as a reminder, this was a college professor. Gross.). Much of this came from his work to mingle the philosophies of Marx with another German, Sigmund Freud. He was also convinced that society was brainwashing people into accepting society's domination by keeping them wealthy enough to not care and to prevent "actual" political discourse from happening (this "actual" discourse being accepting a communist revolution).[35] In fact, Marcuse hated the idea of toleration of ideas, calling it "repressive tolerance," saying that the way it was used, in a blanket and equal fashion, meant that "official" ideas were superior.[36] In his own words:

Within the framework of such a social structure, tolerance can be safely practiced and proclaimed. It is of two kinds:

1. the passive toleration of entrenched and established attitudes and ideas even if their damaging effect on man and nature is evident, and
2. the active, official tolerance granted to the Right as well as to the Left, to movements of aggression as well as to movements of peace, to the

party of hate as well as to that of humanity I call this non-partisan tolerance "abstract" or "pure" inasmuch as it refrains from taking sides—but in doing so it actually protects the already established machinery of discrimination.[37]

If you're wondering where the Leftist professors blatantly accusing the Right of being about "hate" rather than "humanity" came from, look no further. Marcuse's solution was "liberating tolerance." Again, in his own words:

Liberating tolerance, then, would mean intolerance against movements from the Right and toleration of movements from the Left. As to the scope of this tolerance and intolerance: . . . it would extend to the stage of action as well as of discussion and propaganda, of deed as well as of word . . .

. . . it must begin with stopping the words and images which feed this consciousness. To be sure, this is censorship, even precensorship, but openly directed against the more or less hidden censorship that permeates the free media.[38]

In other words, Marcuse has a standard for tolerance. It's a double-standard, and he advocates for "precensorship" to prevent you from even *thinking* of anything he considers "regressive," which he identifies with the political Right and "the self-styled conservatives."

"Withdrawal of tolerance from regressive movements before they can become active; intolerance even toward thought, opinion, and word, and finally, intolerance in the opposite direction, that is, toward the self-styled conservatives, to the political Right—" I'll stop. Now we understand why Christianity today is the most-persecuted religion on college campuses and in the broader popular culture, why prayer left public schools, and why many naive Christian young people enter college faithful only to leave as mentally ill fornicators. It's not good, but it is to be expected when "everything that exists must perish" is your demonically aligned priority.

And it gets worse. Now, we should also note that Marcuse's "extend to the state of action" wasn't referring to protest. It was referring to violence (which, according to Marcuse, we *must* tolerate on the Left, while quashing even the attempt at Right-leaning thought.)[39] It's a real mask-off moment.

He justifies it by saying we're about to collapse into a Rightist tyranny, so he has every right to be the tyrant first. He's the good guy, after all. This is why violence and coercion targeting conservative Christians has become normalized—and often isn't even prosecuted. Meanwhile, communism has crept into schools, from primary through postgraduate, and Christians surrendered even the life sciences. Instead of the sanctity of human life, generations of students have been taught that life arose by chance, holds no eternal meaning beyond itself, and it's all just a struggle for the fittest to survive. What a bleak worldview, and yet, that is exactly what the Darwinian origin story taught to our young people is. Note that Charles Darwin and Karl Marx were contemporaries. The seeds of anti-Christian academia were sowed a century prior. Alleged "scientific facts" have replaced the pursuit of truth. And there's one more character from history we have to thank for that.

The last member of our unholy Marxist disciple trinity is not European but Brazilian. Paulo Freire was born in Recife, Brazil, and was a devotee of Marx, Hegel (Marx's own philosophical-mystic inspiration), and Gramsci, among others, and he's the one responsible for much of our current difficulty, thanks to his development of "critical pedagogy," also called critical theory.[40]

Freire wanted to make education something completely different than it was. Remember the Seven Liberal Arts and the Socratic Method? Things designed to train you how to think? Freire recast that as a "banking model" of education, a kind of colonialism. It perpetuates a kind of "false consciousness" as Marx would have it; in other words, education actually brainwashes you into accepting the current (non-Marxist) order of things.[41]

What Freire advises is a reciprocal relationship between a teacher and a student where they're both equal learners, with the main point of education not to merely impart knowledge, but to embark the students on a process he called "Conscientização,"[42] sometimes translated as "Conscientization."[43] This is very much in line with the idea of Marxian "class consciousness" and involves teaching people to view themselves in terms of their marginalization as a way to wake up from internalized false consciousness.[44]

The goal of culturally Marxist education, then, is to inculcate this "conscientização" in school lessons. In other words, Freire's teaching method wasn't about merely teaching Marxist doctrine, but turning education into a Marxist radicalization engine. He didn't teach Marxism; he taught how to think in Marxist terms.[45]

"But Dr. Ingle," you might say, "this is just some nutjob from South

America. Surely he didn't have any impact on education!" Unfortunately, Freire's vision has impacted influential politicians, scholars, and educators. And, his most famous book, *Pedagogy of the Oppressed* is one of the most influential education texts in the world.[46]

Summary: How College Became Communist

Tying it all together now, we have in the ancient world academic excellence equating to mentorship, logic, and an enlightened citizenry. As time went on, and amid the rise of Christianity, the university began to look more and more like a proto version of the modern college campus. But the focus remained on the development of the whole person and their intellect, with special attention placed on Christian ethics and doctrine. Universities were meant to be the place of truth, where qualified learners could continue their education and become upstanding, contributing citizens of society—and, of course, stronger Christians.

And then the one-two punch of the Napoleonic Wars and the Industrial Revolution changed everything. First, the Prussians wanted an obedient, submissive populace; then, factory owners did, too. Those make for the best assembly line employees and factory workers, after all. Then in rebellion to everything that reminded him of capitalism, Karl Marx attacked the entire system; communism means all oppressors must go. His *Communist Manifesto* focused on the economic consequences of imperialism and industrialization, but his disciples put a sociocultural spin on his philosophy and infiltrated American institutions, from federal bureaucracy to Hollywood to, of course, academia. And as a result, culture now comes with communism by default. The "long march" through education is complete; the Christian foundation of the university has been torn apart.

By 1969, only 27 percent of professors self-identified as conservative, falling to 12 percent by 1999.[47] As of this writing in 2025, it's 8 percent and declining.[48] At elite institutions, one-in-three professors identify as *atheist*,[49] compared to making up just 4 percent of the general population.[50] Contrast that with the explicitly Christian nature of university staff in the olden days! Indoctrination is inevitable unless you choose very carefully.

But it gets worse. Going back to the Prussian school, that system is responsible for creating what we now know as the credit hour. The credit hour measures time spent under lecturing: just put a student in a classroom, then measure their education by how much time they spent being lectured. This might come as no surprise, but the Soviet Union's Red Army applied this same concept to brainwashing the formerly-imperial Russian Army. Every single soldier had to spend a minimum of three hours being propagandized with communism. That was the baseline. All their training had to stop—no more firearms training, military strategy and tactics, and calisthenics—you had to sit in a classroom for ideological indoctrination.

It gets crazier. When the GI Bill was passed—and the US government first started paying for veterans' college after World War II—the mechanism they used was the credit hour. They granted universities money based on how many credit hours they were teaching. Not based on quality. Not based on outcomes. Just on credit hours. The system evolved during the "Great Society" under President Lyndon B. Johnson into what we now know as the Pell Grant and student loan system. What began happening then was this: College degree programs began creeping up. You could give a degree at 120 credit hours. But the average degree program became 160 credit hours. Why? Because the government was paying by the credit hour! It's price inflation! And so the Marxist administrators of universities nationwide realized, in effect, *'Hey, we can extend the length of the degree . . . which now means if you're going at a reasonable pace, you're graduating in six years instead of four.'* And because it's all based on credit hours, students were saddled with even more debt. But who bought all the student debt? The federal government did, during the 2008 financial crisis under President Barack Obama.

So there's a clear throughline: The college debt crisis we have today stems from communism entering the college system. The communists made college more expensive and burdened an entire generation with debt. And of course they did; because who owns that debt? The federal government. So now, you're intellectually propagandized to obey the state and financially obligated to obey the state. Unfortunately, this affects even explicitly Christian (and private) universities, which I've observed experiencing a "mission drift" even during my career. Many colleges of various denominations have shifted over time from truth-first to tuition-first. In other words, if standing for a specific truth such as the Biblical definition of marriage could be deemed offensive to faculty or students, no stand is taken; truth is surrendered. To paraphrase Marx, just a little bit of wokeness on a Christian college campus will eventually cause "everything" Biblical on that campus, in class and in coursework, to "perish."

From the Prussian school system to Pell Grants. What a ride through history that was. Now, with that over with, let's return to the present, to the university campus specifically, and follow what happens to a poor conservative college student named Dave. It's his first day of his freshman year, and boy will it be a ride.

CHAPTER 3
WHAT HAPPENS WHEN CONSERVATIVE STUDENTS GET A LIBERAL EDUCATION

IT'S ORIENTATION DAY AT NORTH SOUTH STATE UNIVERSITY, and for Dave, it's the first day of the rest of his life.

You know Dave. You've met him before. Maybe he's your nephew, or your daughter's boyfriend, or the good kid next door. Real salt-of-the-earth kind of guy. Raised right, by two parents who did all the right things. Took him to church on Sunday, youth group on Wednesday, football practice on Monday and Thursday.

If you were to ask Dave what his politics were, he'd blink, and be silent for a bit. He's not out-of-touch, but politics isn't exactly the biggest thing on his mind. Maybe it's the cheerleader he has a crush on, or maybe he's a bit anxious about his math test. And sure, he'd get into a debate with his classmates once or twice, but he'd rather be out with his friends after school;

what Republicans and Democrats are doing in Washington doesn't really matter to him down in the middle of Nebraska.

But if you asked again, he'd probably say that he's some sort of conservative, like his parents were. Maybe he'd be a bit rebellious and say libertarian, just to be different. Thing is, Mom and Pop weren't really invested in making sure their son was a hard-nosed political conservative. They wanted him to be a good, kind person, who keeps his promises, who does the right thing, no matter the cost. And in that respect, they succeeded. Everyone who knows Dave –whether they're his teachers or his fellow classmates or the people at his church—all say the same thing about him. "Oh, he's such a nice young man!"

Sure, Dave had his quarrels with his parents; what teenager didn't? But he didn't get into anything dangerous, no criminal activity, no drugs, nothing of that sort. Just your average growing pains for a teen desperate for some freedom and autonomy. His parents figure that college will give him that. It'll be good for him. Small-town Nebraska might be too small for him, they think. Moving to the city for a bit, getting somewhere new, that'll help. And of course, Mom and Pop drive him down and help set up his dorm.

But now he's at North South State University, taking his first steps on the campus. Alone. Free.

In many respects, it's everything he ever wanted. Dave can do whatever he wants. Even skip classes (but he would never!) if he was prepared to face the consequences. And so he has two options. He could continue to live and hold to the values of his parents, imported from Heartland, Nebraska. Or he could try and reinvent himself, figure out *who he really is.*

Some small part of him wants the change. After all, that's what all the books and movies and TV shows make college out to be. Parties, drama, but ultimately in the end, finding yourself. Frankly, the degree is secondary, in these stories.

But what the stories didn't show was that colleges know that students are eager to experiment, to push boundaries, to "find themselves," and to take some unwise risks to do so. Students' identities are in flux, fragile, *vulnerable.* And behind every other door, there's a Leftist propagandist masquerading as a professor, salivating over the prospect of "helping" these students find themselves. Helping find the "best" version of themselves.

Helping find the Leftist within.

Shaping the Mind

"Train up a child in the way he should go; and when he is old, he will not depart from it."[1] So says the Bible, and I'm not about to argue with it. It's true, but when parents trust in what they had taught their sons and daughters, I fear they're neglecting one crucial fact.

When you hand your child over to a university –or worse, send them across the country into an unfamiliar land, alone with no support system– you're giving them into the hands of leftist professors, and giving the academic environment the next stage of training. And, unfortunately, your children will not depart from *that*.

Your child's teenage years are some of the most formative of their lives. They're starting to figure out who they are, and are often reaching for independence.[2] This is often where they're solidifying their personality, and forming their own beliefs.[3] Some of these were significant changes to things like conscientiousness and emotional stability.[4] These changes often coincide with the brain beginning to "rewire" itself, a process that doesn't conclude until around age 25.[5]

Now, factor in the other stresses of college life to this developing mind. For many students, they're far away from home, and not on a vacation with their parents; it's their first time living on their own, and independence has its own burdens. And consider the culture; how many movies and TV shows portray college life as a unique chance at self-discovery? This is, in many cases, the script that freshmen approach the university with.

What does this mean? Students who show up to college are *uniquely vulnerable*. They're not just at an age where their personalities are finally solidifying, but even their brains are still reworking themselves. They're in unfamiliar territory, often exposed to new ideas and new ways of life.

And the fact that some people who call themselves teachers and professors would take advantage of that sickens me. But it happens all across the country.

How does it happen to Dave?

Well, Dave is trying to figure out exactly what it is he wants to do. I've seen it plenty of times, where incoming freshmen don't quite know what they are going to major in. For Dave, let's say that he was interested in engineering, but also economics, and after a long time considering it, decided to pursue a BA in economics.

So on his first day, he was excited to see his new class. He had signed up for economics classes, but also, as per the advice of his academic counselor, he included a few General Education classes, the kind of courses that universities make everyone take in an attempt to ape the "well-rounded" classical curricula of the past.

His first class, Introduction to Microeconomics, isn't that bad. The teacher is a little odd, sure, not quite up to date with how PowerPoint works, but he spends his time explaining how supply and demand curves work. Pretty simple, basic stuff. He *does* throw in a few examples about how oil companies are screwing over the environment that doesn't *quite* fit with the lecture, but Dave just shrugs that off.

The problems came with his second class, what was ostensibly a history class. It was supposed to be on colonial history in the Americas, which was actually a period that Dave found fascinating; he liked hearing stories about the pilgrims at Plymouth, or the Boston Tea Party. But instead, the professor focused all of her attention on the atrocities that the English colonists committed against the natives. And, of course, a whole unit on the 1619 Project, which the professor says is legitimately one of the most groundbreaking works of historical research.

Now, on occasion, Dave would have heard his father listening to talk radio. But Dave had been much more interested in listening to his music, so all he was left with was a mild sense of unease. What the teacher was saying felt wrong . . . but then again, she was the professor. Of course she would know better.

He had taken another Gen Ed class after that, this one on English literature, specifically women's literature. But it wasn't just that, of course. Most of the class was about bashing men. How men excluded women from literature. How men make spaces hostile to women. How men objectify women.

At first, Dave wanted to push back. But she was the professor, after all . . . and come to think of it, he *had* said some crude things about some of the cheerleaders when he was in high school, talking with his football teammates in the locker room. Maybe he *was* part of the problem. Maybe there *was* a point to this. He begins to doubt.

Let's take a step back. What happens to a young, impressionable conservative Christian mind when exposed to overwhelming amounts of liberalism, Marxism, atheism, third and fourth wave feminism, and queer theory?

Some of them begin to accept it. From a common sense standpoint, it figures. Students are in an unfamiliar place, and their authority figures—the professors—preach their leftist beliefs as if they're well-established facts. If a student doesn't know what to expect, if their parents don't warn them about the insane bias that they will encounter, then they're more likely to just imbibe leftist doctrine wholesale as fact.

This, of course, is why communists love the "seat time" and "credit hour" approach to education. If you spend enough time teaching something to someone, you begin to accept it. It's not just about the content; it's the structure of education that starts to warp students. Tell a lie from a position of perceived authority long enough, and people will believe it.

All this trends with what we're seeing in polling. Pew Research has reported that over the past few years, the presence of a college degree has been a source of division. Just under half of people with college degrees end up reporting liberal political views, and for those with postgraduate (Masters and Doctorate degree holders), it's over half. With no college experience, those reporting conservative and liberal views are overall equal.[6]

Take a look at the infographic below.

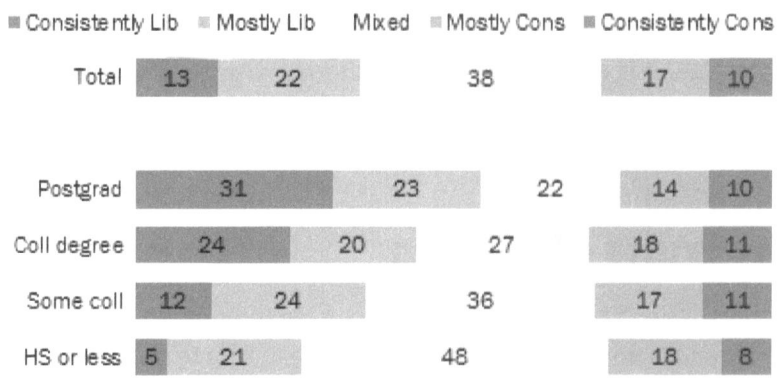

One of the things you want to notice is that while there is a bit of variety in the amount of people who have "consistently conservative" views, it's very small, between 8 percent and 11 percent. "Mostly conservative" results were likewise a stable amount, between 14 percent and 18 percent. [7]

But liberal answers? At the lowest amount of education (High School or less), 5 percent for "consistently liberal," and 21 percent for "mostly conservative." But every step above that, those numbers increase . . . but only for the "consistently liberal" (AKA the hardline left) numbers, going from 5 percent to a whopping 31 percent at postgraduate level. Think about that. With high school education or less, hardline left views (or hardline left views according to however Pew Research measured them) made up a twentieth of the group. At postgraduate education, it's just under a third.[8]

While we would need a statistician to officially prove it, common sense tells us a few things. One, the amount of conservatives doesn't change by more than five percentage points overall. Two, the amount of people who are "mostly liberal" rather than "consistently liberal" doesn't change that much (ranging from 20 percent to 24 percent). Three, the "consistently liberal" amount grows as the amount of education grows. And four, the group that shrinks is not primarily conservatives, but the "mixed" view group, ranging from 48 percent in those with High School or less down to a minimal 22 percent among postgraduates.[9]

In other words, being more educated doesn't make you less conservative; what appears to be happening is that among those who are liberal or mixed, the more education one receives, the more liberal they become. It's not that conservatism is opposed to education (otherwise we'd see the numbers go down), but that college *radicalizes* people.

So, let's see what this does to poor Dave.

The Fruits of Leftism

It's been a few years, and man have they been rough on our Dave.

He ended up switching majors, from economics to sociology. He enjoyed learning about other cultures, but found that the things he was learning about –how society was set up to privilege people like him (straight white Christian men), how society was keeping women and people of color down, how his religion had been the cause of so much suffering and misery– left him feeling bewildered. Guilty. Angry.

And when he tried to share this with his family, well . . . he wasn't sure what he had expected, but their reactions were part annoyance and part confusion. Dave wanted to share what had *really* happened to the natives at Thanksgiving, how his professor had explained that *actually,* Thanksgiving was celebrating a *literal genocide,* but nobody wanted to listen.

It was exactly what his teachers had warned. His parents were too invested in whiteness and narratives of colonialism; they couldn't actually be reached by any conversation, otherwise they would just have agreed.

He hadn't gone as far as one of his classmates, who had proudly announced that her parents were hideous racists and sexists, and that the only thing she could do was cut them out of her life completely. That had shaken Dave. *Would he have to do that?* He hasn't. Yet. But he has distanced himself from them. They don't listen when he tries to explain what he had learned, about how all white people participate in upholding structures of racism in society. "Willful ignorance," his professors had explained.

Dave had stopped going to church as well. It just . . . didn't feel right. His youth pastor had warned him about atheist professors. He had seen *God's Not Dead.* This, at least, he was prepared for, whenever the atheist professor tried to explain why God wasn't real. But . . . that never came.

Instead, he had learned about the atrocities committed by Christian missionaries in the New World (even that term is offensively Eurocentric, his teachers said). Dave had been prepared to argue that Christianity was true, when his professors said it was false . . . but they didn't seem to care about true or false. It was harmful, they said. An outgrowth of Empire. A way to enforce whiteness onto natives and erase their culture.

The pastor at the local church would say, "Go and make disciples of all nations," at the end of his sermon, and the next day, Dave would learn about how missionaries were themselves an arm of colonialism, and efforts to convert are acts of colonialist violence. How could he believe, after what he had learned? How could he remain complicit?

At this point, Dave had become his childfree sociology professor's offspring.

It's a tragedy we see every day, and it stems from an unlikely source; reproduction. As the saying goes, the right reproduces sexually, while the left reproduces mimetically. Conservatives see their children as their children, and your children as your children. Leftists by contrast, see your children as their children; in fact, it's probably best that you get out of the way so they can raise your kids properly.

We see this in birth rates. While it's been long-known that red states have higher birth rates than blue states, this trend even goes down to cities. The average woman in more conservative Dallas will have 2.23 children, while the average woman in more liberal Seattle will have 0.96 kids in her lifetime.[10]

Elon Musk calls it the "woke mind virus," and he's more right than one might think in terms of that slogan.[11] Leftism reproduces itself not by growing families, but by infecting healthy hosts. Jordan Peterson compares it to parasites feasting on a beached whale carcass, as leftists squander the institutional capital they inherited.[12]

> . . . Harvard was a treasured place—but simultaneously something ripe, in consequence, for the plunder. The same might be said in a somewhat lesser and typically understated and tentative Canadian manner of McGill or the University of Toronto or the dozen or so of our major centers of once-international-quality advanced education. The parasites—flying, without exception, the flags of the radical left—began to make their appearance and plot their takeover during the turn on tune in drop out hippie 1960s (a mantra developed at the very Department of Psychology I later served in at Harvard itself).[13]

What had started as a vaunted institution meant to help develop students into fuller human beings has now become a breeding ground for terminally immiserated leftists.

But maybe that's a small price to pay for gainful employment. Maybe you can just pinch your nose until you get a job. Unfortunately, I've bad news for you (and for Dave)—even that pipeline has broken.

Let's see what went wrong.

CHAPTER 4
HOW THE COLLEGE-TO-CAREER PIPELINE BROKE

IT'S GRADUATION DAY AT NORTH SOUTH STATE UNIVERSITY, AND for Dave, it's the first day of the rest of his life . . . again. Unfortunately for him, he's not only been sold a bill of goods with regards to the rampant Leftism, but also the more practical matter of employment. And while employment was the last thing on his mind when he was crossing the stage to get his diploma, Dave had constantly been assured that his bachelor's degree in sociology would translate to a steady job and a nice fat paycheck. After all, when he was in high school, his guidance counselor showed him a Bureau of Labor Statistics print-out that "sociology majors earn a six-figure salary."[1]

But a few months out from graduation, no such $100,000-plus job offers have come. And now Dave is using his sociology degree to socialize with customers at his local chain coffee shop. He's in a rough spot, thanks to this breakdown between college promises and job market realities. And it's almost making all of the rants his professors delivered about "capitalist exploitation" seem even more prescient. He's *educated*. He's got a *degree*. But he can't find any work actually doing what he's been educated for, work he was promised for years now. It's what his parents assumed (and in fairness, it was more accurate in their time.) It's what high school assured him (who's going to disagree with the government when you, too, are the government!) And of course, it's what professors and university administration assured him, that everything he had been learning in the classroom would be immediately applicable to a job.

Unfortunately, just like gender studies nonsense or the "elegant" Marxist theories as fragile as hothouse flowers, the "applicability" of many undergraduate courses cannot survive contact with the outside world. Even aside from the anti-Christian, anti-American indoctrination that modern campuses foist on their students, many are still selling a lie. Not only are most secular colleges delivering what they did *not* promise (and what most sane people *do not want* for their children), they're not even delivering on what they *did* promise (which is why people might tolerate the indoctrination in the first place). **They're not delivering the jobs that people wanted!**

You've probably heard of the term *unemployment*, so let me (re)introduce you to the term *underemployment*—"college graduates working in a job where less than half of the workers have at least a bachelor's degree."[2] In other words, they're working jobs that they didn't need to get a college degree to achieve. In fact, 35 percent of recent college graduates are underemployed, whereas only about 25 percent of older graduates are underemployed.[3] Other sources have found that more than *half* of all graduates are underemployed after the first year of graduation. And after a decade, that only decreases to 45 percent. And worse yet, underemployment seems to trap those involved; very few people go from college-level employment to underemployment, and those who start out after college underemployed are far more likely to be there after a decade.[4] Barista may be Dave's day job; it just might have to become his dream job.

The chronic underemployment trend also isn't evenly distributed among education backgrounds; "harder" disciplines like computer science or engineering have less underemployment than liberal-arts-focused subjects like marketing or, of course, sociology.[5] But college entrance processes don't come with honest disclaimers as to which degrees are more likely to get you properly employed compared to underemployed. Perhaps the sociology and business schools would see a sudden drop in enrollment if they told the truth. Outside sources have done a lot of work in sharing this kind of information, but institutions often fail to publish it.[6] Follow the money.

Speaking of money, the only thing that seems to alleviate underemployment risk (apart from the choice in more quantitative degrees) is **internships**. In other words, real life experience.[7] In fact, it's an almost 50 percent *lower* chance of being underemployed when there's a paid internship.[8] Yet not even *one-third* of college graduates complete a paid internship.[9] The one factor that has a major effect on avoiding underemployment, and most colleges and universities seem to just . . . not care. Not require it. Not push for it. Not reach out to businesses as a regular part of their duties, like we do at Southeastern; here, we require internships as a core part of every degree program, and we work with local businesses to secure those opportunities for our students. But others just . . . expect things to work out for people like Dave who didn't know any better,

You know what they say . . . "If you fail to plan, you plan to fail." So why have colleges planned to fail in connecting students to the jobs they need? Why have they decided to abandon getting students the very thing they signed up to college for? Let's find out.

Where It Went Off the Rails

While college officially promises a degree (if you make it through the "rigors" of their "education"), there is the implicit "well-paying job" guarantee on the other side of that degree. Students know this, their parents know this. And so do the faculty at such institutions. So, how do the faculty rate themselves?

A Gallup poll from 2014 informed us hoi polloi that "A whopping 96 percent of chief academic officers at higher education institutions say their institution is "very or somewhat" effective at preparing students for the world of work."[10] How very sure of themselves! At least you have to give them an A for confidence. But where did the general public sit? Well, according to that same poll, only 14 percent of Americans strongly agreed that colleges were preparing their students for workplace success.[11] Obviously, over a decade ago, the academic world lost the faith of the public.

But what about business leaders? The ones hiring? The ones exposed to the graduates in question? How many strongly agreed that the newest crop of students had the necessary skills and were "well-prepared"[12] to enter the job market? Eleven percent.[13]

They're even *lower* than the general public. What that tells me is that the average American isn't pessimistic *enough* on how well college is preparing their students. The people hiring new students are even *more* disappointed.

Among Southeastern University administrators, we talk a lot about the fact that college is disconnected from the context that education should occur in; this is why we put so much effort to bring Southeastern "into context." We believe that your campus should be the place from which you intend to begin work. We are an outlier. As Gallup summarizes, "The biggest problem is that no one really knows, because the level of intentional collaboration between higher education and employers is downright pathetic at the moment . . . there is certainly no evidence that leaders in higher education are taking this work seriously or that employers see it as mission-critical to the future of our country, nor is it being brought to great scale."[14] It tries to be fair in blaming businesses, too, but they're far more aligned to the general public's opinion. And that Gallup piece was 2014. That was before we saw the madness on our college campuses explode, from the various 2020 riots to those in 2024 and 2025, with violence and mayhem ratcheting up with each installment. How much worse has it gotten since?

And *why*? What's changed so drastically that it's caused faculty to not only isolate themselves from businesses but from reality itself?

Now-President Donald Trump campaigned on many things, chief among them being his promise to "Drain the Swamp!" The Administrative State—what some call "the Deep State"—had been growing at an astronomical rate. Laws reproduced like cockroaches in the dark corners of the executive branch, unbound by the checks and balances meant to curtail excessive law-making (as they're not in the legislative branch).

Decisions were not being made by those elected to make those decisions but by unelected bureaucrats to handle all of the regulations "needed" by the various Agencies and Departments, bureaucrats ultimately not answering to voters. And for a country whose revolution started with cries of "No Taxation Without Representation!" and "No Kings But King Jesus," another others, well . . . lets just say the idea of a large swath of the government being unaccountable bureaucrats anointing themselves with kingly powers and inflicting their will upon people who never consented has rubbed a majority of the American people the wrong way.

Unfortunately, many secular colleges have a similar problem. The size of the non-teaching faculty has been swelling. We college administrators aren't hiring more professors, mind you. It's the administrative departments.

Yale, lately, has more administrators than students! These aren't teacher aides either; these are people whose only purpose is to perpetuate the administrative departments, and they've sucked up to a quarter of the entire budget, often being better compensated than the professors (the ones whose expertise you actually want). And their job? Informing committees about the decisions made by other committees.[15]

This is a good point to note the impact of legislation on the administration of state colleges. The more regulations that the Department of Education placed on higher education, the more the administrative structure grew to accommodate it. Higher ed is not simply greedy; it's enabled to be and demanded to be. A perfect example of this were Title IV offices. Prior to 2010, there were no Title IV offices. But a "dear colleague" letter from the Department of Education—not even an official statute—forced colleges to have to hire armies of pseudo-lawyers to enforce what metastasized from protecting against on-campus sexual assaults, to enforcing gender ideology. The cost burden was significant. That's why we can trace $0.27 of every $1 of tuition right back to federal regulations. And so, administration goes—not because it needs to.

Since 1976 up to 2018, the number of full-time administrators in college has not only doubled, but nearly tripled, at a 168 percent increase. The number of other professionals (not counting actual faculty) grew by 452 percent, whereas neither faculty nor actual student enrollment even doubled, much less kept up.[16] The administrative department has metastasized, with seemingly no end in sight. And it's not administrators behind it; it's the federal government.

The Endless Grift

Like so many bloated NGOs and non-profits making headlines lately, the federal government doesn't exist to serve the people who fund it—taxpayers, citizens, voters, even veterans—but to perpetuate itself. Administration. Bureaucracy. Inefficiency. Academia has, in many ways, had to keep up. And so we get a sprawling, parasitic federal ecosystem that siphons money, energy, and trust from the very people it's supposed to help. It creates problems faster than it can pretend to solve them, and then demands more funding to fix the mess it made. Here's how this federally overextended system ultimately harms all stakeholders in academia. Because it's not about blaming individuals, it's about the incentives everyone has to play by and for.

The Students

Students are treated as if they're so fragile that the slightest bother might traumatize them, thus they are set up to fail. We've discussed how they're taught nonsense from professors, but what they're *not* taught—these so-called "soft skills" like punctuality and professionalism—also hurts them. They're going into a world unprepared to provide what employers value, and the working model of life they've been given—where anything emotionally distressing requires days off work, and lateness, and therapy—make them liabilities. All of this while they're not engaging with internships and being taught propaganda rather than truth.

Professors

We've been harsh regarding professors, and some of them have quite a bit to answer for. But a few of them are well-intentioned and want to teach well. That said, most don't want to adjust to any new business models to improve themselves; they want to lecture on the same thing they've always lectured, then go home while their teaching assistants do everything else. The laxness of discipline often makes classrooms hard to control, and they simply don't want to deal with it. Watching universities shrug at tardiness or plagiarism or other violations of the school's code of conduct has to be demoralizing.

Parents

When students start college, it's their parents, for the most part, paying the exorbitant tuition. While it might seem like they're paying more and more to have their own children propagandized to hate them, they're actually not paying for that. Well, not all for that. Some of that money is going towards the salaries of those useless jobs that populate the administration.

Alumni

These may have it the worst. According to the U.S.News and World Report, the average cost of college tuition for the 2024-2025 school year was $43,505 for private colleges and $24,513 for out-of-state public institutions.[17] And in 2023 alone, a staggering one in four U.S. adults under 40 had student loan debt, according to Pew Research. Their median debt ranged between

$20,000 and $24,999.[18] And what do they get out of it? A degree that many businesses are seeing as a liability, an indicator of emotional instability more than education and competence.

The only ones getting anything out of this situation is the bureaucratic state that set the system up. We have students saddled with debt and crippling anxiety, professors frustrated with an administration that exists solely to jump through all of the hoops that the federal government has set up. There *has* to be a better way to run colleges. Fortunately, there is.

CHAPTER 5
HOW UNIVERSITIES CAN DO BETTER

OS GUINNESS, AUTHOR AND PHILOSOPHER, WRITES ABOUT what he calls "civilizational moments." These are points in history where civilizations are tried, tested, and testify of their claims. They must, in a sense, prove their worth to the world. They must state, "I exist, and it is good that I exist, and here is why."[1]

The price of failure? To be destroyed. Whether that is to be hollowed out, so that another animating ideology, with its own beliefs, its own shibboleths, and its own priorities, takes and changes what is left; or ruined utterly, so that the only place for that civilization is in the dead pages of history books, that depends on how the civilization fails.[2] As Guinness writes:

> Whatever the standpoint and the perspective people take, what is certain is that the West now faces a critical moment and contest. It will either experience a genuine and profound renewal of its ideas and ideals, it will replace those ideas and ideals with different but equally

powerful ones, or it will decline beyond hope of recovery and take its place as the latest entrant in the select circle of history's former great civilisations. All but one of the world's great civilisations are found in history books, ruins, and museums, and it appears that the West—the present exception—may be about to join them.[3]

But what happens on the macro level of entire civilizations, I believe, can echo downstream into the micro level of institutions. Case in point, the subject of this book: higher education. We saw where it started, from Aristotle and Plato to the medieval scholars, broadly animated by a Christian tradition, focusing on freedom of inquiry and the pursuit of knowledge alongside the betterment of the self. We saw where it went wrong, from the tyrannical "innovations" of the Prussian model and the Marxist backlash that turned education into indoctrination into the quasi-religion of Marx. And we saw the breakdown of the efficacy of college, where job placement became rarer and rarer, and underemployment was growing more and more rampant.

The University as an institution is at its own civilizational moment. Economic pressures need it to perform, but the ideals behind it have been hijacked by malcontents, more interested in either promoting their most fashionable form of insanity or just making money (or avoiding upsetting the wrong people). It needs to reorient itself, return to the roots of what it once stood for. The University, as a concept, used to educate and ennoble students, but now it traps them in debt while teaching them useless nonsense. It needs to recalibrate, and for that, institutions need to enact some pretty radical changes to their decayed status quo. Zooming out a bit from college to include the subsequent early years of the workforce, we see that calling and career exist side by side. The college experience should prepare our young people for a career while also helping them discover their God-given calling. There is no division between sacred and secular in the kingdom of heaven. This idea of division is how the world thinks, and, unfortunately, how many Christians also think. Our redesign of the Christian university as I suggest here can fix all of this.

So, where do we start? What steps can colleges take to get back on track, especially Christ-centered colleges?

Be Formative!

There's a strange and dangerous idea floating around Christian higher education today, that we are no longer "allowed" to form students. That means shaping their worldview, instilling virtue, and calling them to a life of truth. But that's deemed inappropriate for conservative colleges—too dogmatic, too directive, too controversial. Isn't that exactly what the other side is absolutely doing? To their students? To our young people?

Secular, even unabashedly Marxist educators sure are. They're forming students daily, shaping their values, their beliefs, and their sense of right and wrong. And they're not subtle about it. They openly worry about "hate speech" while promoting ideologies that reject the very idea of objective moral order. They shout about inclusivity and tolerance while teaching young people to despise the Christian foundations of Western civilization.

And when we, as Christians, try to stand for truth, they accuse us of doing what they are doing: indoctrinating, projecting, and brainwashing. This is the oldest trick in the radical Left-wing book—accuse your opponent of doing the very thing you are so they'll worry about defending themselves and rejecting even the appearance of doing what you claim they are. That's rough. And so meanwhile, far too many private Christian colleges have thrown up their hands. "We don't teach students what to think," some say, "only how to think." That's not good enough. That's not right. That's not Biblical. We are called to do more than deliver skills and degrees. We are called to form lives.

Between the ages of eighteen and twenty-four, a person is at their most impressionable. These are the years that shape a person's trajectory spiritually, morally, and intellectually—and least of all, professionally. College, like it or not, is the only "adulting" ritual left in American culture. If we Christians believe what we claim to believe, then this is our mission field.

And the mission is clear—form identity around Truth. We live in a society where every day you're bombarded by thousands of "facts" and opinions about how to live your life. Everyone with a phone can now tell you what kind of person you should be, how you should live, and what you should believe.

What's been the result? Greater levels of violence, distrust, and division. Isn't it crazy that in an era of "open information" and "instant connections," 77 percent of Americans believe the country is more divided than ever before?[24]

It's clear from this past year that we are living in a crisis of truth. We need to talk about the results of a study I learned of from a Josh McDowell sermon many years ago. The survey involved more than 200 of what were considered "the most spiritual students" from various churches and denominations

They were asked, "If you were in a negative situation and could escape the consequences by lying, would you lie?"

Out of 209 Christian young people, 204 said yes—most immediately, without hesitation. Of the five who didn't say yes, one young woman said she'd have to pray about it. One young man said, "That's a tough one, but I don't think I would." Only three students said "no."

The researchers then expanded the group to 313 students and asked, "Do you believe lying is wrong?"

310 out of 313 said yes.

Then they asked, "Why is lying wrong?"

Almost all responded, "Because my parents taught me it was wrong."

Now, that might sound like a good answer. It's not. If morality is based solely on what your parents taught you, then you've just justified every evil in human history. You've justified the Holocaust because someone's Nazi parents taught them it was right. You've justified racism, white supremacy, and substance abuse because if right and wrong is just what your parents said, then there's no moral standard higher than upbringing.

Anyway, the surveyors then asked, "How did your parents teach you?"

Almost half of the students couldn't go beyond that question.

Fifty-five percent said, "Because the Bible says you shouldn't lie."

So the researchers followed up with, "Why does the Bible say you shouldn't lie?"

Out of all 313 students, only three could answer.

What does this tell us? It's not enough to know whether something is right or wrong; you must know why. The Bible teaches that personal transformation begins with truth. Truth is not rooted in rules or principles; truth is rooted in a Person. Killing is wrong not just because the Bible says, "Thou shalt not kill." It's wrong because God is life. Hatred is wrong because God is love. Injustice is wrong because God is just. Impurity is wrong because God is pure.

The basis of right and wrong isn't our parents, our church, our pastor, our educators, or the thousands of voices on social media. It is the very character and nature of God, revealed through Jesus Christ.

If the Christian university does not form this belief, this worldview, in our students, then why are we here? Scripture gives us no excuse for neutrality.

"I am the way, the truth, and the life," Jesus said (John 14:6). We are not free to treat truth as abstract or optional. We are not free to be passive while our students are spiritually and ideologically captured by other voices.

Ephesians 2:10 tells us we are "created in Christ Jesus for good works, which God prepared beforehand, that we should walk in them." And Ephesians 5:9 reminds us that "the fruit of the light consists in all goodness, righteousness, and truth." Our calling is not to avoid offense. Our calling is to love what is good and hate what is evil (Romans 12:9).

That includes reclaiming the conversation around truth from secular academia by us, the Christian university. Yes, we do live in a culture experiencing a crisis of truth. *That's why we're here*. Christian higher education exists precisely to resolve that crisis by integrating faith with learning, experiences, and identity formation.

Think of the conversation between Jesus and Pilate. "What is truth?" Pilate asked. But the answer wasn't a theory; it was a Person, standing right in front of him. Truth is not only objective, it is relational. A relationship with God is what forms the Christian worldview.

Which leads to the most important question every student will ask every week about every subject they study in school: *What do I do with this?*

Christian higher education cannot be afraid to answer that question. It cannot shrink back from worldview formation. In fact, that is the conservative Christian university's most sacred obligation. Because just calling a school "Christian" doesn't mean they're actually forming Christians. And just because you teach about theology doesn't mean you're shaping disciples.

If we believe there is truth—and that Christ is Truth—then we must act like it. Yes, in name, but in curriculum, in culture, and in courage as well.

To put it simply, the purpose of Christian formation during the college years is to help uncover the calling that God has on each student's life. Vocation . . . discovery . . . God's divine design for your life . . . your personal mission . . .

No secular university is going to help believers or non-believers discern their calling. Unfortunately, the Christian campus isn't much better in many cases across America. We can do better, and we must.

Be Affordable!

Pew Research reports that, in 2023, one in four US adults under the age of forty have student loan debt. Let that sink in. A *quarter* of young adults ("young" in this case being merely below forty years old) are going into significant debt for college. For those who have completed just a bachelor's degree, median debt is somewhere between $20,000 and $24,999. For postgrads? That figure lies somewhere between $40,000 and $49,999. And those with student loans are finding it difficult to get by in this economy.[5]

That's the median number, and that's the price of a car. Only, when you go into debt for a car, you actually get something that does what it's advertised to do. As the last chapter showed, colleges and universities are selling themselves as the way to get a good-paying job but are increasingly failing to deliver on that promise. Why is it so expensive?

The US News and World Report says that the average cost of tuition for the 2024-2025 school year was $43,505 for private colleges and $24,513 for out-of-state public institutions. And while that doesn't include scholarships, it also doesn't include room and board, or meal plans, or textbook prices.[6]

Even if a student is getting financial aid in the form of grants and scholarships, which they won't have to pay back, they will still need to go into debt just to afford going to school. Unless their parents have a ton of money set aside (And that US News and World Report tells us that less than half of them feel ready to pay that price), they'll have to sign up for astronomical levels of debt.[7]

The system is working fine . . . if the system is designed to ensnare as many young people into a trap of forever paying creditors and lenders, and never getting back on their feet. If this system was meant to do what it was advertised to do—pay for college—then we're in deep trouble. Or, well, some institutions.

At Southeastern University, we're moving away from this old, outdated model. As its president, I'm proud to say that we're innovating how we learn, and more importantly, how we end up charging for college. While I am committed to upholding the sacred traditions of the university, student debt is hardly what one can consider part of the honorable and treasured history of Western education. And so we experiment.

We're offering alternative payment schedules, like subscriptions, rather than traditional tuition. And while SEU focuses on more traditional degrees, we've also branched out into offering trade programs and certification for things like software development, data science, and cybersecurity. We've also launched hundreds of partner sites around the US, allowing students to learn in their local communities. This can slash tuition by up to two thirds.

But the thing I'm most proud of is our SEU Ministry Network. For those students pursuing careers in ministry, we have partnered with churches all across the country to bring education off-campus. These Network Campuses integrate hands-on ministry *practica* in areas such as worship, youth, children's ministry, production, and creative arts. Students typically serve 12-15 hours per week under the guidance of a local ministry leader and graduate with approximately 4,000 hours of ministry experience. Leadership is cultivated through this real-world service, consistent feedback, and intentional mentorship.

While our Ministry Network is unique, other schools are experimenting with online learning. Both the State University of New York (SUNY) and San Jose State University (SJSU) are experimenting with massive open online courses (MOOCs). One student could take a MOOC class for only $150, rather than the in-person $1,700. And while the goal is to make them free, there would be a small price paid for enrolled students so they can be credited to a student's educational record.[8]

Be Relevant!

The exorbitant price isn't the only thing that makes college a losing proposition for a lot of people. As the last chapter demonstrated, college isn't offering the benefits it used to. We sold degrees as tickets to high-paying jobs, but now most students are underemployed.

Colleges need to prioritize job placement for every major and "market" these majors to students *before* they enroll, to reset societal expectations for that question "what do you want to be when you grow up?"

While we can talk all day about the noble duties that universities have to better students, we also have to deal with the dirty reality of business. There needs to be a return on investment, specifically by degrees granting jobs or work opportunities that graduates would not have gotten if not for their education. Colleges have to be as dynamic as the job market.

Political campaigns have made free college into a buzzword, and it's understandable why. Student debt is a massive issue, and it's often overwhelming to the people who have it. But it isn't the answer. As a college president, when I hear "free education," I can't help but see the gaping holes in these extravagant promises. The decline of college enrollment, it turns out, is less based on financial reasons, and far more dependent on the fact that students and parents lack the appropriate tools to make the most of this experience.

I'm the president of a college, so while you can say that I have an interest in how college is paid for, you also have to say that I have a unique vantage point on the issue, one that gives me insights to the struggles of students that pundits don't see. I can't help but see the gaping holes in these extravagant promises of "free" college, because while the issue of debt is a *critical* part of this conversation, it is still a critical *part* of the conversation. We also need a solution to this growing trend of students struggling to find work and purpose because they were unable to gain an actual education. And in this case, an education that ends with employment.

Colleges are graduating students with no real-world experience, burdening both the student (who now has to scramble to find anything that will pay the bills) and prospective employers (whose crop of potential new hires are woefully unprepared). In fact, according to some surveys, 58 percent of employers think newer graduates are unprepared for the workforce, while 38 percent of employers actively avoid hiring them. And this makes sense, given that almost half of said employers needed to fire an employee that had recently graduated, and that one in five of them had had the awkward experience of the graduate bringing a *parent* along to a job interview.[9]

For the parents reading this book, this has to be unthinkable. But this is the world we live in now. Students are not just leaving college without the hard skills needed for a job, but even lacking the soft skills and awareness of basic things like "don't bring a parent to your job interview."

If we want our students to succeed in this environment, we need to change our idea of what college education entails. It's no longer enough for students to just sit in classrooms for hundreds of hours a semester; employers look at that and just see a lack of hands-on experience. If we want students to find jobs, then we need to find ways to get them that experience.

At Southeastern University, we have implemented several policies to help prepare our students for their careers now, while they're still in school. We offer experiential learning opportunities, both inside and outside of the classroom. Whether this is working with career liaisons or taking advantage of our Ministry Network, we're constantly pushing our students to get experience.

We also prioritize learning the "soft skills" that are so helpful in gaining employment. Beyond just organizing events and VIP days with prospective employers, our Career Services team also offers more in-depth coaching. We do mock interviews, so that students can practice before applying for an actual job, and get used to the experience so that they don't feel the need to bring their parents along. We critique resumes, so that students can note the most relevant skills for the employer they're trying to attract. And we also have Professionalism Education, so we can teach those social skills that students are sorely lacking.

Other schools are starting to jump upon this pattern. Most colleges have career centers, aimed at career placement. They often host job fairs, though those are becoming less common. Now, how much this is promoted to the student body is a different question, but other colleges are following suit.[10]

Internships are also becoming more popular, and many schools are requiring them to graduate. Career centers also end up helping students find *paid* internships, which most certainly helps weed out predatory businesses.[11]

In fact, at SEU, all of our bachelor's degrees now also include required practicum hours, where students leave the classroom and get hands-on experience working in their intended career field. We also offer trades programs where students can complete an apprenticeship and experience on-the-job training alongside their traditional education. And just over the last six years, our students have completed more than six million hours of relevant internship experience that have given them the experience employers are looking for and help them land jobs after graduation.

Be Focused!

It's one thing to demand a better way for paying for college, or for an education experience more geared towards job placement. But that does not address the rot at the center of the current conundrum. Students are not learning. They're being indoctrinated.

We covered in extensive detail where the university started in previous chapters. But think back to Plato. Even with his ideas of philosopher-kings, his Academy was a place of academic freedom; the most Plato ever intervened was to suggest problems for the scholars of his time to solve.

When we go forward in time, to the Middle Ages, you had a focus on the seven Liberal Arts not as a way to enforce conformity, but rather to expand a person's mind, and ennoble them to pursue medicine or law. They taught *how* to think, rather than *what* to think.

That changed, as we noted later, with Marx and his disciples; Gramsci, Marcuse, and Freire. They turned education from a process of ennoblement and expansion of the mind to a form of religious induction. Rather than teach necessary skills and knowledge, they focused on making sure every student walked away thinking like a Marxist.

We at SEU are opposed to this.

We make no apologies or excuses for what we are—an explicitly Christian organization. That fact, which we state outright, means we do not have to hide agendas or disguise our beliefs. While we are a Christ-centered community, that we are explicit in our desire to nourish the soul and to aid our students in character development allows us to actually focus on learning.

Colleges need to refocus on actual academic excellence. When there's an implicit, hidden goal of indoctrinating students into Marxist thought, the goal of the university shifts from education to conversion. The purpose of a thing is what it does, remember? So, if the actual goal is conversion, then academics will suffer.

It's a simple fix. Reorient back to actual education. Go away from humanities departments that are obsessed with interpreting Shakespeare or Dante through a feminist or queer lens. Something like St. John's College's Great Books program, for example, where students go through the influential thinkers of Western Civilization and actually engage with the best of our culture's thought.[12]

If the university does the previous two suggestions –slashing its prices and focusing on job placement– but doesn't fix the more significant problem of mis-orientation, then the remedy will only be a temporary band-aid. The biggest problem is the one written about ad nauseam by conservative pundits, and for good reason; universities are malfunctioning because they're not educating first and foremost. Not all of them, but a good many.

At the moment, however, you can only control what you do. And if we're going to be doing our best to live out the conservative Christian case for higher education, we best be prepared for the reality of college as it is now.

CHAPTER 6
HOW TO PREPARE FOR COLLEGE LONG BEFORE COLLEGE

SO, THE TIME HAS COME TO START PREPARING YOUR STUDENT—or yourself—to find a good college. There's a lot up to chance, and oftentimes, as we've discovered, the deck may be stacked against you. Colleges are getting busted for illegal admissions practices to favor people of some races over others when it comes to enrollment (to the point where the US Department of Education needs to get involved),[1] and even as some of these laws are repealed, schools are clinging to their outdated and bigoted practices.

What strategy can you and the young person in your life pursue? My advice to parents—always—is to focus on what you can do to make your child as attractive as possible for college admissions. While there may be unfair practices for some schools, colleges are also looking for what they can guess are surefire graduates. Think about it; if you're a college administrator, do you want the student with a low test score, a bad grade record, and a lack of participation in extracurriculars, who is more likely than not to flunk out (and thus you lose out on all that future tuition money), or do you want the student with stellar academics, high test scores, and plenty of after-school activities to write about (who is much more likely to keep paying)?

While there's a lot that's just up to chance for college admissions, one of the key items you can influence is the SAT or ACT score your child earns. And, if your child is considering graduate school, then the GRE will matter a lot more.

Finding advice on the test itself is easy enough. Walk into Barnes & Noble, and there's whole sections of SAT or ACT prep. Or you can look online if you don't wish to pay. But the one piece of advice I would give is what we do at Southeastern University, with our Career Services with interviews: Simulate the test. You can get practice tests for your child easily enough. However, when your son or daughter sits down to work through it . . . don't just have them go through it. Simulate the test environment. No phone, no distractions. Make it as much like the test as possible. And then do it again, and again, and again.

We all can get nervous, but it's repeated exposure to nerve-wracking situations that calms those nerves. Get your kid used to the testing environment, so when the day comes, it's not a completely new experience. And while there will be some pressure, enough practice sessions can ease the stress that need not be there.

But after the test, there's more choices to make.

Choosing a School

Christian parents and their children have a difficult task ahead of themselves. Most universities today do not reflect the values their children were raised with, the values these parents believe in, or the values these students try to uphold. And this isn't just mere ambivalence to those values; many institutions are places where Biblical truth is seen as oppressive, and must be challenged at every opportunity.

Wokeness, to them, is the religion that must replace your child's Christian faith. From dorm life to the classroom, everything reflects this. Holding moral standards is considered strange or prudish at best. Truth is relative, unless it's about a progressive shibboleth, and then it is inviolate. Faith is mocked, unless it's a strain of progressive Christianity so anemic it can't even insist on the existence of God, but can insist on the importance of social justice.

What do you think happens in a school like this? Even if your child doesn't fall away, it's still a bad environment to be in. In young believers, you get deep confusion and isolation, when they should be using this time to cultivate their faith. For families who have invested years in nurturing their child's faith, it is disheartening to send them into an environment that may pull them away from it.

What college your child chooses *matters*. And not just in terms of academics or career. What about your son's conviction? Your daughter's faith? Your child's calling? How do you approach this decision?

First, know that not all colleges are out there to make your child an apostate. Colleges and universities are not neutral, but are shaped by ideologies, philosophies, and worldviews that color not just what is taught, but how it is taught, what is permitted, and what is forbidden, on campus.

Look for colleges that clearly uphold Biblical truth, not just in the classroom, but in their leadership and in the campus culture. Make sure the college's mission, their vision, and their values align with what you want your child to grow up under. The institution is coming alongside you, in a sense. If a school can't clearly articulate its stance on faith and culture, that's a red flag.

Don't settle for your convictions merely being tolerated. They should be encouraged.

Second, ask the tough questions before saying "Yes" to anything. Before you make any final decision, make sure you have the answers that really matter. And hint, those answers aren't about football teams.

Are the professors aligned with the university's faith commitments? It's a good sign if a college has a statement of faith, sure . . . but that ultimately means nothing if the professorate doesn't follow through. What does it profit you if the Dean of the College of Business is a committed Christian if the entire economics department is staffed with Marxist professors? Do you think Christ or Karl Marx will be centered in those classes?

Does student life reflect Christian values or just use Christian language? Again, faith statements are good . . . so long as they have teeth. So long as the college is actually committed to them. It's easy enough to dress up the secular hedonistic chaos of modern student life in Christian-ese, but it's a lot harder to fake living it.

How does the university handle today's most pressing cultural issues? In other words, *does this school stick to its guns when push comes to shove?* If you have a faith statement saying that they adhere to Biblical sexuality, but they roll over and allow men in women's sports, in women's locker rooms, because that's the madness that our current culture endorses, then their stated beliefs are meaningless.

The school's convictions need to go deeper than branding. In our society, with the Marxist "long march through the institutions," many institutions established on a Christian bedrock are now bastions of leftist ideology. These questions should help you unmask those situations.

Third, think *eternally*, not just academically. While college might only last for four years, its effects echo throughout your life. Understand that, and take that into account; chasing prestige or programs isn't worth inviting unwanted influence into your child's life. Choose the place that will help your son or daughter grow in their calling. Choose the school that will strengthen their convictions, that will prepare them to meet the world, and shine with truth in a world so long in the dark it has forgotten what the light looks like.

Your child's future is about more than merely acquiring a degree. They're going to become someone in the process. Where they go for school matters, yes . . . but who they will become matters even more.

Choosing a Major

We've talked before about resetting expectations for that pernicious question, "What do you want to be when you grow up?" While we discussed the college side of things, how they have to better market what the majors actually entail . . . on the consumer side, you still have to do research too.

A lot of students have regrets. According to BestColleges, in fact, 61 percent of graduates wish they could have gone back and changed their major.[2] Four years, potentially wasted, learning skills and knowledge your child is not actually enthusiastic about.

So help them. For your own family, or if you work with young people, help them learn about real professions. And I'm not talking about pushing them to trade school; explain what someone with an economics degree might use it for. Learning about jobs often comes two to four years too late, when students are in the middle of looking for internships or job-shadowing, in the middle of a degree program. By this point the student has wasted time and money on what they *might* want to do.

Students should be focusing on what they want to do in the real world. And if they start early, they can start asking themselves how they can begin doing whatever their calling is, and start making money early.

Choosing your major, then, is important work. And as president of a university, I have some advice I can give. And this I'll give to the students directly.

First, start early. Most four-year colleges start with a year or two of general education (attempting to imitate the Liberal Arts approach of ages past, making sure you're well rounded, and that the engineering students know a bit of literature, and the English majors know some science.) This means you don't need to be locked into a major right away.

This gives you time to look at your options. Browse your school's degree offerings, see what stands out to you. The school will have career counselors and mentors; use them. Or use professors you find yourself connecting to. They might be able to point you in a good direction for your study.

Second, think about what interests you. It might have been in different jobs. Or volunteer experiences, or clubs, or classes back in school. Maybe it was history—you really dug that project in 10th grade about the Civil War, and liked digging into records to touch history first hand. Maybe it was writing essays—you might have been part of the student paper. All of these could be good indicators for what careers might appeal to you.

While your major will have required courses, you'll have to fill credit hours with electives. Start taking some from different areas of study to see what interests you. Branch out, try new things. You might land on the thing that really connects with you, and pushes you towards your potential career.

Third, start researching career paths directly. Once you've had some time to think and figure out what your interests are, start looking into career options. Start with the Bureau of Labor Statistics; they have websites like CareerOneStop that have up to date stats on career availability, and what those pay.

Other websites like Zippia and Gladeo can help you explore careers by interest, major, and even personality type. Look around a bit, and see what stands out to you. And once you know what career interests you, work backwards–what degree requirements exist for this field? Then, pick a college major that matches.

Fourth, talk to professionals. Those already in the field, like visiting employers or even other professors, will have valuable insights as to what knowledge is useful to have. Prepping by making a list of questions to ask is never a bad idea. Meet with these professionals for a cup of coffee, or after class. Their insights into what it's like in the field, and how they got to where they are, will be great guidelines for what path—and what college major—you might want to take.

Finally, think about doing an internship. If you're not sure what you want to do, then maybe volunteering might help. Maybe you want to go into teaching; volunteer as a teacher's assistant for a professor. Maybe volunteer at a local church, or apply for an internship with a local business. That first-hand experience will help you feel confident about your choice. And that will help you figure out if your college major is a good fit.

Apply Thoughtfully

When you're helping your child apply for colleges, there are a few things you can do to help. And while a lot of the work would be done beforehand, with stacking extracurriculars, acing the SAT or ACT, and keeping that GPA up, there are a few things you can do to give your child better chances during the actual hiring process.

First, be realistic. While ambition isn't a bad thing to have, and you no doubt think your child is the best in the class, use the metrics from the SAT and GPA. Gauge their actual achievements as dispassionately as possible; I'm sure you think they should be in Yale, but if they don't measure up to the criteria (or price tag), then by not having realistic aims, you're setting them up to fail.

But while you're doing this, make sure to check what scholarships are available that your child may be eligible for. A lot of schools have high tuition costs, but then offer a wide variety of scholarships to offset that. Take advantage of these!

Second, make sure to be thorough. When your child is submitting for college admission, they might be required to submit other things. Art schools, for example, often require you to submit a portfolio of your work. Extracurriculars might require extra documentation. You do not want your child being passed over because they forgot to add a certificate. It never hurts to double-check your work.

Lastly, make sure your child is actually doing the work. In this day and age, there's the easy temptation to use ChatGPT to write admissions essays or submit everything. Not only does this rob the student of a chance for real reflection (or, well, as much reflection as one can get out of a college admissions essay), but it also has a good chance of setting them up for rejection. AI often messes up, whether that's from hallucinations or misunderstanding the prompts. And when it comes to admissions essays, there's a good chance ChatGPT's vague waffling will, at best, not inspire any admissions admin, if not clue them in and deliberately reject the admission outright.

Optional: Utilize State 529 Plans

This may be a bit late for some of you, who are just getting ready to send your kid off to college, but for those of you who are reading this before you have kids, or have young children, listen up.

State 529 plans are tax-free (if you use it solely for qualified educations), and available for anyone. This is the kind of thing you can have the grandparents and aunts and uncles all contribute towards. Every little bit counts, and even if you think it's too late, the benefits are still, in my estimate, worth it.

If you can start earlier, however, you, your parents, your grandparents, can use this 529 plan to make college as debt free as possible.

Now, I can't go into a ton of detail about these, as each state has different requirements for 529 plans, but this is the kind of financial tool you should research or talk to your financial advisor.

So with all of the advice in this chapter, let's move on to what happens when your child gets accepted into college. There's four years of learning ahead, not counting grad school. Let's make sure those years count.

CHAPTER 7
GETTING EVERYTHING WE CAN OUT OF THE COLLEGE EXPERIENCE

HOW MANY MOVIES START OFF WITH THE MAIN CHARACTER going off to college? I'm honestly not sure of the answer, but I know why it is so popular. Those first days of college are chaotic whirlwinds of students rushing around to sign up for classes, to make new friends, and to attend orientation. And that's all supposed to happen in that first week.

Nerves, excitement . . . That's what we expect the average college student to feel. Your child might be nervous, but so will everyone else be nervous. Maybe they're uncertain about their classes, or about the homework load, or whether their professors are nice. Or maybe they'll be more practical-minded and try to chart out the best parking spot and quickest route to the classroom.

But you can help your young student with this first week. What we want is for them to drop into college not so nerve-wracked and worried they didn't prepare enough they can't function, but also not so nonchalant that they won't be prepared for everything. They need a battleplan.

First Week Battleplan

The first week of a college semester is a crucial time to prepare. A lot of classes will be quite different from each other; Introduction to Macroeconomics might start with a brief overview of the syllabus, while something like Introduction to Creative Writing might start with expectations for workshops and ice-breaker exercises, while your boring Engineering Materials class will be all about the syllabus and grades for the first week. And, if you're on a campus, there's a good chance these classes are going to be scattered across different buildings.

But your student can get a headstart, even with all this guesswork.

First, they can prepare for their classes ahead of time. Those first few weeks of class can be a rather confusing mess, but your student will have their syllabi for their various courses. These will have lists of materials (e.g. a calculus class may require a graphing calculator while an art class may require you to buy paints or pencils) and, more importantly, textbooks. Your student can purchase those before the class starts. These may also have course calendars or assignments to complete early.

And when your student does go to class, it can be hard to know what to expect. So . . . be overprepared. Notebooks, binders, pens, laptops, phones, textbooks . . . The worst thing that might happen is a professor says everything is on paper, so please put away phones and laptops.

Second, your student can get familiar with the campus layout ahead of time. There's nothing worse than running late for a class and *not knowing* where the classroom is. Orientation tours can help, but your student will have more free time on their hands than before; encourage them to explore and figure out where everything is. Even after the first week, it still pays for your student to figure out where the student center, the library, and other important sites are located.

Finally, encourage your young student to prioritize keeping up with both their academic and personal lives. It's easy to fall behind in the first few weeks of a semester. Show them how to budget their schedules to allow for a few extra minutes in a commute. Don't put essays and assignments off until the last minute. Planning is excellent, but you won't be there to prompt your student to take breaks, so practicing holding onto a schedule early on is an excellent strategy.

Scheduling will also depend in a large part on the living situation.

Routines will be pretty easy to handle if your student is living on campus; they might live right above a dining hall (making a very quick trip for breakfast); the challenge here will be for your student to stick to the schedule. And, of course, handling the other requirements for on-campus housing (such as following all of the rules that the school establishes).

Off-campus is similar, though it might require, if you're in a town or city, a few blocks walk. You may also want to make sure your child is not getting ripped off for rent, if they're renting an apartment nearby, and that the neighborhood is a safe neighborhood. But like on-campus housing, the real trick is to stick to established schedules.

The real challenge comes with when your student lives near home and commutes. You'll have to schedule that commute in, and vehicle maintenance (if they're driving; some schools are near trains or other forms of public transportation.) This also means they need to schedule in time to find parking, and walk from parking to class.

Your student needs to also prioritize eating well, and scheduling in leisure time; all work and no play makes Jack . . . well, stressed out and spiraling after a few weeks. They need to be sleeping enough. And they need to ground themselves in the Word, and prayer. They need to make time for Christ along with time for homework.

The Semester Strategy

Well, you've got your battleplan for first contact with the enemy (the chaos of college life.) But after that . . . What then? College is often a stressful time for students, and so having a longer strategy for handling the rigors of college life is crucial. As a president of a university, I have some advice to offer.

First, teach your children how to study. Many high school students aren't prepared for the academic level of college coursework. Often, the kid who doesn't have to study for tests, who can just listen to a class and remember everything, ends up blindsided. Talk with your student and encourage them to change their scenery by studying in various locations and discovering what study techniques work best for them. And above all, make sure they know the importance of budgeting out time, rather than cramming the night before.

And while there might be one or two times it makes sense to skip classes . . . it should not become a habit. They're paying a huge sum of money to learn from their professors; playing hooky isn't just foolish, it's a waste of (partially your) money!

Second, remind your student to utilize on-campus services. Make sure they are aware of what resources they have access to, in the university's library or the student center when it comes to studying. But not just studying. If they're struggling with stress or anxiety, they have resources at their fingertips to use. Universities offer everything from academic assistance through tutoring centers to services in wellness, counseling and physical health.

Let them know it's okay to ask for help. Asking for support is not a sign of weakness, but a sign of humility.

Third, encourage your students to interact with their fellow students. Classroom settings can be unfamiliar, a little threatening. But having friends can help overcome some of that initial anxiety. As students get to know their fellow classmates, they are more likely to participate in class discussions and be a part of study groups.

Motivate your student to get out of their comfort zone and get to know the people in their classes. Once they start taking classes in their major, these friendships develop lifelong bonds that might help them later down the road. It might even help to share stories of your own friends made in college.

And don't just encourage them to connect to professors. Getting to know their professors enriches their education experience; it is also helpful later down the road when they need a recommendation from a professor for a job or scholarship. One of the things I myself benefited from was personal connections I made with faculty members outside of classes. Some professors will be advisors or sponsors to college clubs and organizations, so if you participate in these you may be able to connect in a more relaxed, social environment. Do not neglect even the simple act of just asking to meet with a professor who may not be in your major's department or even at your school.

Fourth, help your student plan out healthy diets and workout routines. While a lot of students might intellectually know that nutrition and exercise is important, they don't really realize it until they transition from a diet of fast food and a workout of couch sitting to something that resembles a well-balanced meal and hitting the gym at least three times a week and find that the stress has just melted off.

Be sure to take your student to check out the gym on campus and the various features it offers. Maybe start a fitness accountability challenge with them, or encourage them to use those group workouts. Talk to your student about what types of foods they should eat daily. Encourage them to take advantage of the cafeteria and the healthy options they offer, like salad bars, fruit, and protein stations.

Fifth, show them the essentials of being an adult. Your child will be living on their own and will have to be responsible for themselves. And first of all, they *need* to learn to handle their finances. Encourage them to set a monthly budget, including all of their expenses from snacks to personal hygiene to essential groceries, and to stick to that budget.

They'll also have to learn to care for themselves—from cleaning their own room and making their own meals to doing their own laundry. If they don't know how to do their laundry, this is the perfect time to teach your child.

Sixth, train them on how to respond to emails professionally. Once your student receives their school email address, make sure they set that up with an app on their phone, so they can frequently check their emails. Share how important it is to keep up, as professors often use email as their primary mode of communication. Your student should also know how to address their professors in emails, using a formal title like Dr., Ms., Mr. or Professor. Emails they send to their teachers shouldn't be as casual as the ones they send to their classmates.

Seventh, keep communication channels open. Now, striking a good balance is tricky. You want to be there for them (and most importantly, you want them to know that fact), but you don't want to be a helicopter parent (and absolutely do *not* call the school because they didn't immediately pick up.) Always pick up *their* phone calls and respond to their text messages in a timely manner. When they are going through something, listen intently, but give advice when they ask for it.

Every child is different, and your son or daughter will naturally gravitate towards some means of communication more than others. Some might want to call, others are fine with the occasional text. You can be a friend for them to rely on, but you also should encourage them to make new friends; constantly calling you means they're missing out on a major part of the college experience. And of course, remind them that they are always welcome to come home for a weekend or during a break.

Mental Health Management

Right now, students need that support, as they're going through what can only be called a mental health crisis. Wiley reports that a staggering 80 percent of today's students are experiencing mental health issues. Of those surveyed, 59 percent of college students reported dealing with anxiety and 43 percent are experiencing depression.[1] Recent reports also show that many students are experiencing increased PTSD symptoms.[2]

And it's only gotten worse throughout the years. Between 2020 and 2021 alone, college students experienced a staggering 50 percent increase in mental health issues compared to 2013.[3] And nowadays, 58 percent of college students report that their mental and physical health is only continuing to decline.[4]

Now, you might be asking yourself what you can do in the face of all of this catastrophe. But by being proactive, supportive, and understanding, you can make a difference in one particular student's life: yours. Your involvement can provide the emotional foundation they need to navigate this challenging period successfully.

A recent United Healthcare study revealed that as students transition from high school to college, their mental health problems (including suicidal ideation and intent) increase by as much as 50 percent. Many of them also experience a relational disconnect from their parents, leading to differences in perceptions of their mental health. In other words, parents don't see exactly how their children are doing.[5]

It's a touchy subject, and it can be awkward to bring up. So, how do you do it?

Well, you may have to initiate that conversation. It's hard, and the data shows that oftentimes, students just don't talk about it with their parents. 46 percent of students report talking with their parents about their mental health once a year or less according to the United Healthcare study. Comparatively, 43 percent of high schoolers report discussing mental health at least twice a month.[6]

And it's not that these conversations don't help; 55 percent of students who talked with their parents twice a month or more felt supported, and having more frequent conversations about their mental health leads to better outcomes for students. In comparison, only 13 percent of students who spoke to their parents once a year or less about their mental health felt supported.

College can be a difficult time, and those initial few weeks of transition, it helps to regularly check in with your student about their mental health. It lets them feel seen, heard, supported. And by reaching out, not only do you show that care and support, you encourage them to be honest with you, so they don't feel like they have to hide from you.

You also need to be understanding. Only 42 percent of college students received help for their mental health issues. Alarmingly, 14 percent of them reported it was because they were concerned about their parents finding out. When they did talk to their parents, nearly one in four felt misunderstood.[7]

Whether you think their feelings are justified or not, you still have to show empathy and understanding for their emotional turmoil. Many of them already feel that they shouldn't be feeling the way that they are, so your doubts or assertions that they are overreacting will only lead them to feel more isolated and misunderstood.

Actively listening is key here. Don't immediately provide them with answers, or assert your opinions on what they should or shouldn't do or how they should or shouldn't be feeling. Instead, understanding what emotions they're feeling, and how it's affecting their personal and academic life will show actual care for *them*. If your student is opening up to you, sharing their struggles, honor that. Your judgements will only hurt your relationship and break that trust. They are likely already feeling ashamed or thinking they let you down, so assure them that you are not upset and that they have not disappointed you. Assure them that you're proud of them for opening up.

And lastly, address their concerns directly. As many as eight out of 10 students are afraid their mental health will affect their ability to graduate on time. Their top stressors fueling this belief include financial concerns, academic pressures, and social or family pressures.

And what does this give us? 51 percent of college students are considering delaying their graduation to cope, and 58 percent of college students cite declining mental health as a main reason to consider taking a gap year or dropping out of college.[8] There's plenty of reasons to take a gap year, but fearing you won't be able to handle the stress should not be one of them. And mental stress should not be the reason someone drops out of college.

As a parent, you must address these concerns with your student. Much of their anxiety comes from fear of the unknown — they are afraid of how you will react if their grades are affected or their graduation date is delayed. This uncertainty will only compound their stress and anxiety over time and isolate them further.

So nip that fear in the bud. Talk to them about these worst-case scenarios. Shift the focus away from expecting perfect grades or seeing their graduation dates as the end all be all. In fact, assure them that you will not be upset or disappointed in them if they need to delay their graduation date. Quell your student's fear, remind them that your love and support for them does not solely rely on their performance or lack thereof. They're your child, after all.

But beyond defanging fear of the unknown, be sure to discuss the other issues with them as well, whether they're practical and tangible (like finances) or emotional (like anxiety or fear of failure.) Is there anything you can do to help them? After all, you love them no matter what.

But if your student is away, out of the house, or even out of state, then you might not be able to do everything. One of the best things you can do for them is encourage them to get help. Many colleges offer free virtual or in-person counseling for students, yet studies show that only 14 percent of college students report taking advantage of these services.[9]

If your student is struggling financially and feels they can't afford therapy, remind them of these resources, or even offer to help pay for their counseling. Churches may have support networks they can tap into as well.

And speaking of churches . . .

Finding a Church

In the flurry of packing lists, meal plans, class schedules, and late-night study sessions, one of the most critical components of your student's college experience often gets sidelined—belonging to a local church. But for students attending a Christ-centered university, involvement in a local church should never be treated as supplemental, optional, or alternative to however else they could spend their Sundays.

Again, the purpose of Christian higher education is beyond academic; it is formational. A conviction we hold among Southeastern University leadership is that the Christian university exists to serve the Church—that is, the Body of Christ. Our college is thus not here to replace it, compete with it, or provide a four-year alternative to it with Sundays' on-campus chapel services, which is why we've made a conscious decision not to hold chapel on Sundays. We want our students engaged in the local churches around us. We want them serving in kids' ministries, singing on praise and worship teams, stacking chairs, preparing after-service meals, praying in the community, evangelizing, and receiving pastoral mentorship from leaders who are walking the walk with them week to week. Yes, we do believe chapel is important, and we have incredible chapel experiences. But your college is not your church. The local church as a branch of the global Church is God's primary plan for the discipleship of souls, for believer-to-believer accountability, for kingdom-building missions, and for spiritual maturing.

The college years are spiritually decisive. This is the first time many students are out on their own, making decisions about how to spend their Sundays, where to find fellowship, and whether they will prioritize spiritual habits (or not, or never again.) If we don't make it clear to our young people that belonging in (and to) a church matters, secular culture will make it clear to them that it doesn't. After all, 66 percent of Americans under thirty in a recent survey who had attended church in their youth quit going after turning eighteen.[10] It's not the age; it's the transition. What do most eighteen-year-olds do? Start college, or at the very least, they leave the routine of adolescence. How you train up a child is how they will train themselves—this matters most in the final formative period that is early adulthood.

To the parents reading: Please consider helping your student find a local church early, even before classes start. Sit down with them, look at options together, map out distances and safe itineraries, visit websites, and talk to pastors. Encourage your child to pick and commit—no church-hopping, ideally.

And for students reading this (perhaps because your parents asked you to): You're probably going to love your campus ministry. You may attend chapel and even Bible studies faithfully. But don't mistake these for a real church; don't settle for spiritual nourishment from peers. Find older spiritual leadership. Join a church. Serve. Worship. Belong. Long after your textbooks are returned, your assignments are submitted, and the old graduation cap is tossed in the air, that local church will still be there.

Speaking of graduation, we need to talk about that—and what happens next, practically speaking. The apostle Paul was a tentmaker, after all, serving in *the* Church but also earning a living out in the world. Let's focus on that next.

CHAPTER 8
▄ HOW TO FINISH SCHOOL STRONG AND GET A BEST FIRST REAL JOB ▄

HIGH SCHOOL GRADUATION IS THE FIRST DAY OF THE REST of life. Now comes the next stage in their life. Job-searching. Your child's or student's (or your!) next goal is to find employment, and they've got a pretty tough economy to navigate. Their passions and gifts led to a college where they felt they could both learn and flourish as a person. And, we hope, a part of their college decision was finding a school with a good record of graduates finding quality jobs in their career fields. They're going to need that record. They're going to need all the help they can get in the end.

Most students across America are ultimately leaving the campus with their cap and gown, their diploma, and—unless they're among the handful that were either gifted enough to earn a full scholarship or well-off enough that their parents could outright pay for everything—a lot of student debt. While there's a bit of a grace period where repayment isn't required immediately, this is something that can crush the student's chances of launching their adult lives if it goes unpaid, so finding gainful employment is priority number one to take care of that.

But the default outcome isn't a cushy job that lets your student pay that loan off nice and quickly. It's five years or more of underemployment, if not actual unemployment, and a perpetual, ever-stressful scramble to make ends meet. Not exactly a great proposition, is it?

Now, not only does this affect the student, but it could affect their family. And I don't mean you, the parent or educator. It might be hard to think about now, as you look at your student, studying for their high school finals, but they may be coming out of college with a significant other. It probably is a bit odd to think about, while you look at your sixteen or seventeen year old son or daughter studying for their SAT.

But it could happen. For example, your son might meet a cute girl in his engineering class, and things might get serious. Or your daughter might be at a student event and run into the guy who ends up being "the one." They might leave their graduation with a serious boyfriend or girlfriend, or even a fiance. Or your student might leave with a husband or wife.

The employment crisis makes it even more difficult for them in this case. The West is suffering a fertility crisis as well, and no small part of that is because raising a family is far too expensive. People are delaying having kids and forming families because they're underemployed and can't afford even a modest house. And one of the new parents staying home to take care of the baby? For many young people, that's unthinkable in this economy!

This is unfortunately a bigger problem for women than men. Men can have kids at pretty much any time, while women are on a much stricter timeframe. If they have student debt, these women will need to work full-time for a very long time. And if they are blessed with a husband and a child … it's bittersweet at best, and more likely to be stressful, because they can't afford to stay at home to raise the child. I heard a story this week about a marketing communications professional who worked until the morning she went into labor. Three months to the day later, she put her infant in full-time childcare and missed the baby's entire infancy from then on until the first birthday. Then her company fired her.

All these things I'm presenting to you right now are a lot to deal with. But it *can* be managed. I just want to make the gravity of the situation clear, and show that the quest for a job after college has real, meaningful consequences.

Finding a job is usually hard work; your student should prepare themselves for long hours and days of researching and filling out applications, often with little to show for it when the sun goes down. But one thing can make it so much more difficult, and that is not knowing where to start, or even where to aim. You can't hit a target you can't see, after all.

Your student needs to run the numbers on what they want to do with their lives. You can help them, but they need to do it; you can't just take care of this for them. What does their lifestyle cost each month? Each year? For the next five years? How can they budget for this?

What are their dreams? Their goals? Their ambitions? And, more to the point, how do you get to be near accomplishing those goals? These aren't rhetorical questions; your student ought to write down what their goals and dreams in life are, and then start figuring out ways to get there. If it's a concrete path, with actual steps that aren't vague ideas like "get educated," then they can start to move themselves into that path. And, by running the numbers, you can make sure your son or daughter doesn't go broke in the process.

Maybe it's about breaking into an industry. Chart out a path. *This* company or type of business often works with *that* type of business, so you might be able to work there and then leverage that experience into being mentored, and prepared for the field. Today's labor market is in constant flux, so in your student's career, they may find many ways to use their skills, and those skills may be a great match for a job in an industry that might come out of left field. Being open to new opportunities, in these changing times, is more and more important with every day.

Finding the Job

When looking for a job, attitude may be the most important factor. It's easy to get overwhelmed, but I always take comfort in God's Word, especially Matthew 6:31-34. To paraphrase, do not be anxious and fearful; God is watching out for you.

Outside-the-box thinking here is an advantage; anything might be able to turn into a job opportunity. Your student should be alert at all times to clues that may lead to a job, and be disciplined in looking for work, and stay self-aware. When they know their gifts, their strengths, then they know which opportunities to look for.

Now, as bad as being unemployed would be, don't encourage your son or daughter to get desperate and go for *any* job that comes their way. They need to learn how to evaluate potential employers. Make sure they ask themselves:

- Will this job allow me to display my talents?
- What are the tasks and expectations? Do they align with my talents, education, skill set, and experience?
- What does the employer want to accomplish through this position?
- Do the company's values align with my values?

Just like how college can shape the person you become, the work you do will influence who you grow to be. But don't just be critical. This is the time to dream! Who would they like to work with? Start with employers in the area, region, and state where your child's college is located—then go national, maybe even international. Have them learn as much as they can about each company and create a file for future reference, or start following those companies on social media. When the opportunity arises, encourage them to make direct contact.

Many colleges offer on-campus resources to help students enter the workforce after graduation, from mock interviews to resume workshops to networking events. Also consider encouraging your student to reach out to people in their desired field, such as past professors, trusted mentors or acquaintances still working in the industry. The people they make connections with at university can be more important than they realize at the time. They often have more insights, drawing from their years of experience, and are able to point you in the right direction for potential employment.

The alumni from your student's school may really want to help them find work. Those alumni were in their shoes awhile back, and they understand the rat race of job-hunting. There should be a database on campus that can give your child names of alums in their career field. Encourage them to meet and network with as many alumni as possible when they are on campus for homecoming or other alumni-oriented events.

Regarding social media, you can encourage your child to use it to their advantage. Hopefully they have not been too wild and crazy online. This is a good time to start looking at their public social media "face" as though they are a recruiter for a major corporation. And in addition to deleting anything that may give the wrong impression, they can start enhancing their profiles with information that highlights personal qualities, interests, and volunteer activities. An online presence can help them in current and future jobs by allowing employers to see them actively building their portfolios. Just be sure to insist on honesty; if an interviewer catches them in a lie about whitewater rafting that they made up for Instagram, then that interviewer will be wondering what else they made up.

There's a couple sites you could look into as well, to make that direct contact.

- **LinkedIn:** Think of this site as the social media of the professional world. Users can connect with new professionals and coworkers, follow businesses, and post content (including a lot of cringe-worthy quasi-inspirational listicles). Members can attend online seminars or workshops and even apply for jobs. It doesn't hurt to encourage your student to create an account and update it regularly with work experience and education. And it could be a good way to break into a field you don't have any contacts with.

- **Indeed:** This is a direct go-between for companies and job-seekers. Users can upload resumes, search, save and apply for jobs in a number of fields, searching by career and filtering to see benefits and average salaries, along with a list of companies that hire in that field. Companies' salary ranges, industry hiring rates and company reviews by employees . . . these are just some of the insights you can glean from their search function. And Indeed also has a blog featuring resume templates and other helpful content for new graduates.

- **Monster:** This site has numerous tools tailored for new graduates, including a comprehensive, step-by-step walkthrough on how to apply for your first job. Monster takes you through the resume-building and application process with helpful articles and videos for how to succeed in each area. Monster also helps you find a new career through their job search tool. They offer advanced search options that give insights based on your experience, education and desired salary to help narrow down your job search.

But even if your student doesn't get the *ideal* job, there are still strategies you can encourage to leverage that job into a better opportunity. Even if they don't land their dream job right after graduation, there are ways to get relevant experience in the field.

Want to be a copywriter for a major business company? Maybe start a blog. Hoping to own a business? Maybe they should consider working in a small business setting, where they can start getting experience across all aspects of business ownership. Even the smallest task, like filing paperwork or answering phones, can turn into a powerful experience that will bolster your child's resume and help their future business.

Fostering a good relationship with their current employers is always something they can capitalize on later in life. And encourage your student to not stop learning. Maybe they could also take online courses for things like Microsoft Excel. They can still audit classes or pursue licenses or certification, and oftentimes those can be pursued while working a current job.

Now, we've addressed this chapter to the parents of students, whether recently graduated or about to. But what about those situations when it's not the young man or woman going off to college for the first time? What happens when someone is going back?

How do you know if it's worth it to go back?

CHAPTER 9
GOING BACK TO COLLEGE FOR THE VERY FIRST TIME

THROUGHOUT THIS BOOK, I'VE ADDRESSED A LOT OF THE ADVICE to parents of first-time college students. Sometimes, I had addressed parts of this to the students themselves. But there's one group that has been left out, one that rarely makes an appearance in our cultural zeitgeist, whether in TV shows or movies or books. This is the older adult going *back* to school.

Maybe this is you. Maybe your son or daughter has already graduated and managed to land that shiny opportunity, and you're wondering if you too could get that chance. Or maybe you're stuck in a dead-end job, staring down an endless series of the same day playing out over and over, slowly deadening your soul every time. But whatever your situation is, this chapter is for you. But probably not in the way that you think.

I veer off from the common conservative position of being down on college in general. Maybe this is because I'm president of Southeastern University, but I've come to realize that higher education offers a lot of experience and credentials that conservatives ought to take advantage of. And, I always thought that part of losing the culture war was less out of directly losing in conflict and more a conservative retreat from the fight, leaving the left to claim abandoned institutions as victory.

In general, I am much more pro-college than your average conservative. So it may come as some surprise that I am *not* going to universally recommend going back to college as an adult, even if you *think* you want or need to go back.

There are reasons to go back to school for the first time, sure, and we'll discuss that, because yes, sometimes going back to university is the right thing to do. But very often, it's the first thing that people jump to because it's what they're familiar with. *Go to college,* they remember hearing their parents say, and it *kinda* worked. So, why not give it another go?

Degree regret can be a big part of it. Maybe you want to get into computer programming, but don't know where to start, and so the idea of another four year degree is kind of tempting, if only because it provides structure for exploring a subject you know little about. Maybe you got an English degree, or something else that doesn't exactly lend itself towards hireability, and think that going back and getting a BBA in Business Administration might help you with starting that business you've always dreamed of.

The danger here is that while you might be familiar with college, the culture on campus you're likely to encounter will be completely different from the culture you were immersed in when you first went to college. The classes you will take will be radically different from what you had taken ten, twenty, thirty, or even forty years ago.

Or maybe you've not gotten a degree. Your son or daughter was the first in the family to graduate college, and you're starting to think that, although you have your own job, you might benefit from higher education yourself. It's a possibility, sure.

But what I want to encourage you to do is think about other potential options. Sure, college *can* be helpful, but it's often not the right fit for these kinds of situations. Sometimes, trade schools can be the answer, as much as I rag on them. Sometimes, it's simple certification courses. Sometimes, it might be just changing up your employment situation.

Part of the reason that I don't always recommend college to the older generations is that often, the reason for someone pursuing it is out of a dissatisfaction with their employment. And while getting a degree can be useful in facilitating that kind of career pivot, it can often come at great expense (all that student debt still applies, even if you're older), and sometimes it's not worth taking on those expenses or stepping out of the workforce. And sometimes it isn't necessary to effect the job change that the person is *actually* looking for.

College degrees can provide you with better credentials, sure, but very often people mistake what they think they want (a Bachelor's or Master's Degree) for what they actually want (a higher-paying job, or a more fulfilling career.) And the result of that confusion can wreck your personal or financial life if you're not aware of them. Going into debt for tens or even hundred of thousands of dollars, when a $350 certification with a training program paid for by your employer would suffice just as well isn't a wise move. But it's a move often made out of ignorance.

Let's use some hypothetical yet to many people otherwise very relatable examples to explore some of the different options available to you.

Scenario 1: Dave, the Auto Assemblyman

Let's look at Dave. He's in his late forties, and he likes cars. Likes them so much, in fact, that he got a job working as an assemblyman on one of the handful of automotive factories left in the country.

But unfortunately, he's not the fancy engineer working on designing the cars or trucks that his factory churns out. No, he's one of the lower men on the totem pole, working on the floor. It's good work, but the pay isn't that great anymore. He wants to move up, but can't seem to figure out what to do.

Part of him is considering trying to take out a loan and go back to college. A public college, probably, and maybe go for a degree in engineering. He likes to tinker with stuff in his garage when he gets home from work. In fact, he's taking apart an engine in his spare time, with his son, so maybe Mechanical Engineering would be a good fit. A good, solid degree to have to get a better, shinier job in the automotive manufacturing industry

Quite a difficult spot to be in, no? Maybe you're in a similar situation to Dave, in the field you love, but stuck in what seems like a dead-end job that isn't giving you the fulfillment you need. What do you do? Where do you go?

Well, the first thing I would urge Dave to do, and what I would urge you reading this to do, if you find yourself heavily empathizing with Dave, is to not completely discount your employer in this situation. There's a good chance that the employer he wrote off as a "dead end" could help him advance in his career.

The first thing I'd advise Dave to do is to take the time and assess his job and where it sits in the company. What jobs are above it in the corporate hierarchy? What jobs are beside it, on a different track? By figuring out his current position's location in the matrix of the company's structure, he's able to see what paths for advancement exist for him.

Very often, companies want to hire internally. Think about it; if you've ever started a job, don't you remember the lengthy onboarding period? The endless trainings you had to complete? The weeks, or months even, of learning the quirks and idiosyncrasies of the company? Now, if you were promoted or transferred internally, a lot of that will be cut down, and you come into a new job with experience and knowledge about other parts of the company. And more to the point, you're not a gamble, you're a known quantity. *Better the devil HR knows than the devil they don't.*

So Dave looks at his job, and what he finds is that where he wants to be is not in the design department with the engineers. It turns out he actually kind of likes the more hands-on approach, but he'd rather be supervising, working with a team under him than being a mere grunt. And, in all honesty, he doesn't exactly like his own supervisor. That guy, well . . . he tends to go on a bit of a power trip every so often, ordering around his underlings to "make sure they know who's in charge," and that gets old very fast.

At this point, Dave has two options.

The first option is that Dave can work his rear off and do what he can to be noticed at work. He'd aim for high performance, and see if there's anything he can do to earn that supervisory position. He could reach out to his own manager and talk about what it takes, or reach out to HR, or other senior members at work. Does he need certifications? Degrees to be considered? If not, then his goal is clear.

Then there's option two. If Dave wants to move up in the industry, but he doesn't see a path forward in his company, then it's probably in his best interest to reach out to another company. After all, he *has* the experience. Sometimes, the upward motion of someone's career happens externally, if that person's current company isn't interested in promoting them. Their loss, really.

Now, this process changes a little bit if we alter that original scenario. Let's say, rather than Dave wanting to move up within the same career path, he wants to move to the marketing department. A "sideways" transition. Now, there may be some more difficulties with this kind of pivot. There is a chance this might require a degree, but if one of these sideways changes doesn't require it (which, for the sake of this example, we'll assume as well), then what you will need is some training and experience.

This is where those other workers and their experience comes in handy. What Dave does is ask one of his friends in the marketing department to catch lunch with him. Then, over a grilled chicken sandwich, well, he grills his friend. *What kind of things do I need to learn?* he asks. *What skills do I need to sharpen, what kind of software programs do I need to get familiar with?*

Soon, with that judicious use of his lunch breaks, Dave has a solid grasp on what kind of skills he needs to learn in order to best make that transition. That networking will also help him land that job. After all, he's making friends with the people who would eventually hire him.

These kinds of transitions may be easier internally, as like Dave, you'll be able to better network with people in your organization. And, as mentioned before, the familiarity will help ease that transition, and make it easier to justify taking a risk on you transferring to a new department.

Very often, the answer to the dead-end job that people seek isn't found in a four-year commitment to a degree. Instead, it's found by reassessing your options from where you are positioned right now, and charting a course to promotion or internal transfer, or even applying to a competitor firm for a better job and leveraging that hard-earned experience.

Scenario 2: Krista, the Office Worker

Let's move on to Krista, a white-collar desk jockey. Like Dave, she's in her mid-forties, but don't mention that to her face, unless you want a stern glare. She works in an insurance firm, handling a lot of the billing and payments for the agents. Not quite a glorified secretary, but pretty close. "Administrative Assistant" is the technical term for what she is, but she mostly assists the sales representatives.

Oftentimes, as she's organizing yet another list of leads for the salespeople, she looks over to the sales section of the office. Part of her wants to try her hand at it, and frankly, hearing what these people make, she thinks it's worth a try. But what steps should she take to go from glorified secretary to actual insurance sales agent?

At first, she thinks back to her niece, who's working on her own MBA. *Maybe*, Krista thinks to herself, *maybe that's what I need to become a really good insurance sales agent!* And before you know it, she's got a tab open on her computer, looking at local universities. Not spending enough time to distract her from her actual work, of course, but the idea has gotten a hold of her.

The only thing preventing Krista from pulling the trigger on this is that price tag; she'd have to go back into debt to afford this. She and her husband had just finished paying off their student loans a few years ago, and she's kind of dreading bringing this up. Nothing against her husband; she loves the man to death, but money has been tight lately, so this might be just added stress.

Well, before Krista enrolls to try and get her MBA, she ought to look at her own company first. You see, Krista doesn't actually *need* a degree, much less an MBA, to sell insurance. What she needs, instead, is a license.

This is one of the things that so many people don't know to look for. Licenses and certifications often end up being the real requirements behind businesses. And these are legal requirements; you can't sell insurance, in this case, without obtaining for yourself an insurance license.

But here's the thing. You do *not* need to go to college to get an insurance license.

Licenses or certifications require you to study, yes, but oftentimes there exist trainings and courses online that you can take to prepare yourself for the actual measure that would get you the specific credential: the examination. Schools and universities do not hand out insurance licenses; those are administered by the state. Which means you're more likely to have to pay for training online rather than four years of tuition.

There are some cases where not needing a college degree is *technically* true, but in practice you would actually want to go and get a degree. If you wish to become a Certified Public Accountant, for example, you would very much want to get a degree in accounting before attempting to take the CPA exam. If you wish to practice law, for example, you can take the bar examination whenever, but you will have wanted to go to law school before attempting it.

But an insurance producer license? That's a different story.

So where should Krista start?

Honestly, like Dave, she should start by using one of her lunch breaks and reaching out to one of the sales managers. Oftentimes, insurance agencies have training materials that they use; sometimes it's to get other agents licensed in other states, while in other cases, it's there to serve as the "continuing education" that license renewals require. But a simple conversation can point Krista in the right direction in terms of who or what to ask for to get access to this training.

There's a good chance that she won't have to pay for it. A lot of organizations have internal tracks for promotion, and a talk with Krista's manager might be all it takes to shift her onto one of these. But if not, then it's a matter of saving up and studying outside of work.

Krista's own experience working in the industry will help too. If she works in life insurance, or health insurance, then she'll have picked up a bit here and there about the rules and regulations, which can often be the toughest part for studying. And if she has trouble grasping some of the concepts in her course, she can work with a bunch of sales agents. She's got a lot of options to choose from in terms of people to ask.

And then the final test; the actual exam. Krista would probably submit some time off, first to get fingerprinted (a lot of certifications and licenses require a background check), and then later take off time again to go to a testing site. There, she'll put all that studying to good use and hopefully ace that exam.

After that, she can return to work with her head held high, with a fancy new insurance producer's license. Or, if things don't go so well, she reschedules the test for another date and hope her coworkers aren't going to ridicule her too much for it.

A lot of people think that you need an MBA or the equivalent to change jobs. And while there are some careers that require a degree—like medicine—or require so much education it might as well be requiring the degree—like law or accounting—a lot of businesses require certifications that can be studied for in spare time. Or even as part of personal development in that business. Many of these certifications can be gotten by anyone! Even some internships require them, which means that Krista may be taking her exam next to college students a year or two out from graduating. But these certifications don't care whether you've gone through four years of education. They just care if you can pass the test.

Scenario 3: James, the Paralegal

Now, let's visit our final example. His name is James, and he's a paralegal in his early thirties, working at a decent but not too prestigious law firm. He never went to law school, but ended up getting this job while scrambling for an internship, and turns out, he was really good at it. So he stuck with it for years, and he makes good money.

But there's still that lingering dissatisfaction with the job. Now that he's working in a law firm, he *wants* to be a lawyer. He wants to help people, and wants to argue cases in court (he was captain of the debate team ages ago.) But James doesn't have the degree, and he hasn't passed the bar, so he doesn't have the license.

He has to go to law school.

Now, unlike Dave and Krista, James *has* to go to college for law. Not only will no law firm not look at him seriously if his resume doesn't boast a degree from a law school, but the legal education he would miss out on if he didn't go to school would make studying for the bar infinitely harder. Law, like medicine, is one of the handful of careers where a degree is actually necessary.

Unlike Dave and Krista, if I were to give James advice, I *would* encourage him to go back to college. With the other two examples, I exhausted all other options first, and in the process, found less costly paths forward to what they each wanted (for Dave, a raise and advancement in his industry; for Krista, the license she needed to get the job she wanted.) But with James, we can exhaust all other options and find them wanting.

Our strategy with the one path left—college—is then to figure out how to minimize the cost of attending.

James doesn't want to go bankrupt chasing his dream of being a lawyer, and there's a few things he can do when starting enrollment to avoid unnecessary costs.

A lot of colleges will require general education credits, to attempt to make a student well-rounded rather than a pure specialist in their degree's field. One of the things James could do is see which classes and credits he could take at a local community college, and then transfer in and count towards his main degree. That might take some extra research, but James is a paralegal; his entire job is research.

The other main strategy, however, concerns his law firm. James should reach out and ask to see if he can get any financial aid from his employer to go back to school.

It's not always a long-shot; employers like seeing their own employees develop (if they're good places to work, that is), and they often have back-to-school programs as part of employee benefits. There's even the chance that they could pay for all of your tuition. It might require you to agree to work for them afterwards, and this isn't a guarantee that your workplace has these benefits, but you'll never know if you don't ask.

You might even work out an ad-hoc arrangement with your employer. If this is the case, make sure to get it in writing, and don't take it for granted.

While at college, see if you can't also continue your employment part-time. This money can go towards easing the financial burden that you have, as well as making sure you stay employed. You want to show your employer that this generosity isn't a waste of money that gets them nothing, but rather an investment in you.

For James, his employer had a program where they would partially fund tuition for law school. While that didn't include his first year taking care of Gen-Ed classes at his local community college, that tuition was barely a worry to begin with. And, he managed to work with HR to shift to a part-time schedule so he could still help out with his paralegal duties while taking classes. It meant a lot of busy nights, yes, but he was still getting paid, and still staying employed with his law firm.

And then, after he graduated, his employer helped him study for the bar exam. They had programs designed to help applicants study, so James took advantage of those. And, eventually, when he did pass the bar, he had a way in with a law firm that knew him and knew he was dependable.

The Last Resort

It might seem a little counterproductive that I spent most of the chapter of a book about the conservative case *for* college showing examples where going back to college was the wrong thing to do.

But part of the issue is that conservatives, for so long, have made blanket statements about college. "Oh, the universities are just full of leftists, there's no use going there, you won't get an actual education, you'll just get indoctrinated!" While there certainly is a problem with higher education, both on the ideological level of indoctrination and on the more practical level of return on investment, blanket statements like "college is useless" are counterproductive at best, if not deliberately damaging (Think about it: Leftists would love nothing more than for conservatives to completely cede all of higher education and access to cultural institutions to them.)

But the opposite blanket statement, that college is always the right answer, has caused a lot of harm as well. Conservatives have a point when they point to students saddled with debt who probably would have been better served in a trade school. Absolutist blanket statements end up doing more damage.

The conservative Christian case for college is a practical case. Conservatives are realists, rather than idealists; they deal with facts on the ground, with the situation at hand, rather than ideological speculation and working everything out on paper and then trying to make ideology fit their elegant theories. And the fact is, many times, when older people want to go back to college, what they actually want is better achieved by making a few strategic decisions, or aiming to get certified or licensed to get the job they want.

And in the rare handful of cases that returning to college is actually the right option, the main strategy should be to minimize debt and maintain employment. The former means you won't be too far behind others in your field, saddled with loans you have to pay back, and the latter means you won't be like recent graduates scrambling for underemployment so that at least you have a job.

When judging this for yourself, going back to school for the first time is the last resort. Ask yourself: are you going to likely get the job you want anyway? Is there any other way you can pivot or promote to where you want to go? Or is the door truly locked, and the degree is key?

MBAs look good on a resume, sure. But they also come with a very hefty price tag that professional licenses or certifications don't carry. And if you can get the job you want without going into debt, and without going back to college and potentially putting yourself out of the workforce for years, then the only reason you would pursue returning to college is prestige. And prestige doesn't pay the bills.

Now, we've danced around it a bit throughout these chapters, but it's time to discuss the famed alternative for college that conservatives just love to promote.

Let's talk shop. Let's talk about trade schools.

CHAPTER 10
THE TRUTH ABOUT THE TRADES, ASSOCIATE'S DEGREES, AND PROFESSIONAL CERTIFICATIONS

TRADE SCHOOLS. VOCATIONAL TECHNICAL SCHOOLS. Whatever you want to call them, they're big in the news right now, thanks to President Trump, who suggested that they take $3 billion from Harvard and pour that into trade schools, and they've been the main theme that conservatives have been harping on for the past decade at least, if not longer.[1]

Watch a conservative talk show. Pick one. Any one. They get to mocking the insanity pouring out of college campuses, and one of the hosts will say something along the lines of, "You know, this wouldn't happen if half of these people went and learned an honest trade rather than Underwater Feminist Basket-Weaving." It's treated as a panacea, as if invoking the hallowed *Trade School* will free the students in college from indoctrination. It'll exorcise the leftism from the college students!

Mike Rowe, the former *Dirty Jobs* star and current host of *The Way I Heard It* podcast, promotes trade schools. In fact, he works to provide scholarships for trade schools, helping people learn how to become welders or electricians.[2] Good stuff, and I think it's necessary. God bless Mike Rowe.

But like so many things in the conservative media sphere, blanket assumptions about trade schools persist. They're treated as the end-all-be-all that everyone should be pursuing, no matter what. The "answer" to the "problem" of college. And while trade schools are definitely the right answer for some people, they're not the right answer for *all* people.

There's a sort of logic to why they're so heavily promoted. We conservatives tend to not like snobs. We have a bit of a knee-jerk reaction when someone acts as if they're just better than the average Joe, that they know more and thus deserve to tell the Average Joe how to think. We don't like it, it rankles us, and so often we just tend to do the opposite of whatever Mr. Smug and Self-Important tells us to do.

And when you hear cosmopolitan people talk about the trades, you can *hear* the disdain dripping from their voice. The condescension. Nobody would willingly *go* into the trades. They're for the people who flunk out of an *actual* education, the kind of people who can't really *make it* in the world. The kind of people you might call a "basket of deplorables" or "bitter clingers" to their "guns and religion."

The trades are where the dregs of our civilization go, because they couldn't cut it in college—that's how the other side talks about the trades. It's not a different path in life, it's a fate inflicted upon those unfortunate souls too uneducable to make it through four years of college. If you can't get a degree, at least you can go to the vocational tech school. It's a good safety net, at the very least, but I sure hope *my* son or daughter doesn't need to stoop so low.

It makes me sick even writing that out. I don't like the elitist disdain for the trades. Working with your hands, doing an honest day's work - these were the kinds of virtues the pioneers and colonists had when they arrived in America. These were the values and hard-earned skills (updated to the modern day) that built this country, and so the idea that one might willingly disparage the trades is repugnant to me.

In our Christian tradition, work and the trades have a special place. Our Lord was not a sage who sat removed from the world, sheltered from the toils of His day; He was a carpenter. Remember tent-making to support the ministry of the early Church? Labor is a sacred offering to God, and to see it treated as something to be disdained is a tragic sign that we have forgotten our roots.

That said, the conservative reaction to valorize the trades as the best path forward is appreciated but mistaken. Often, the people who laud the trades then go on to disparage those who pursue higher education. They're learning useless information at best, or indoctrinating madness at worst. *What job do they think they're going to get with a Gender Studies degree?*

The answer to elitist snobbery isn't populist snobbery. It's an accurate and measured view of things. Of course, that doesn't sell well in our age of outrage media, but nevertheless, the trades are important. And so is higher education. They should be working together, and the fact that they're viewed as antagonists is a huge part of the problem.

On a cultural level, we need a recalibration. We've discussed at length about how colleges have drifted from their moorings, have secluded themselves in their ivory towers and gotten further and further out of touch with average Americans. Trade schools have luckily escaped that self-alienation.

It might not make sense at first, the fact that I'm making this case. Why would I, the president of a university, support people *not* going to college? Isn't that against my own interest? If I was just selfish, then yes, it would be against my own interests. But I have the conviction that education should serve the whole person: spiritually *and* vocationally. That's why I believe the future of higher education must include the trades not as a fallback, but as a foundation upon which to build your life's calling.

Conservatives are realists. We deal with reality, not ideal conditions dreamed up in a philosopher's white paper. And the fact on the ground is that not every student is called to a traditional, four-year university path. For some of them, the right choice is the trades. It's not because they can't "handle" college, but because they want to—are called to—go into more technical work and are more fit for an apprenticeship than a four-year course. Those who idolize a bachelor's degree may look at them with disdain, but in the end, it's what's best for the student that matters. For some of them, what their hearts and souls need is to be out in the field, working with their hands, rather than sitting behind a desk.

Who Should Go Into the Trades?

Trade schools aren't for everyone, as I've said before, and it bears repeating. Too often has conservative media promoted it indiscriminately. Not saying "this *might* apply to you" but "*everyone* should go to trade school instead of college and learn something useful."

If I've come across as bashing the trades before, it's not intentional. What I want to do is provide a bit of a course-corrective. If college isn't for everyone, then neither are trade schools. If we can celebrate that some people should go into trade schools, then we should celebrate people who should go to college. And, obviously, vice-versa.

But who *should* go into trade school? What kind of characteristics does your student need? What should your child's goals be if a vocational school is their best fit?

I'm going to leave out the obvious virtues of diligence and hard work and responsibility for two reasons. One, other conservative commenters have spoken endlessly about these, and how the trades are better at promoting them than college. But point two, as a counter to point one, these virtues are still needed for college as well. Saying that your son or daughter needs to work hard if they go to a trade school implies, somewhat unfairly, that they don't need to work hard in college. That is very much not the case, and it turns out that diligence is just as good a virtue on a college campus as it is in a workshop.

So what should you be looking for in your child's character to determine if they're a good fit for trade school?

One, they need a clear vocational goal. Your son or daughter needs to know exactly what kind of job they want to do. When going into a trade school, they're not learning general ideas, they're learning how to do a specific job. Does your son or daughter want to work with cars? That's probably not specific enough. Auto mechanic? That's a lot more specific, and it allows you to choose the right classes and career track for your child.

Generally, while trade schools are cheaper than college, it's not a place to be shopping around trying to figure out what you want to do. So if your son or daughter doesn't quite know what they want to do with their life, taking the time to explore careers before committing to trade school is a must.

Two, the vocation a student wants to commit to is the kind that fits a trade school. If your son wants to be an accountant or doctor, for example, then trade school is not the right fit. Again, that's not a problem. We need skilled doctors just as much as we need skilled electricians. But if they want to enter the trades, if that's their calling, then you need to find a trade school that offers the training or apprenticeship specific to what they're looking for. Something *close* won't cut it.

Three, the student should actually enjoy the work to an extent. It can still be hard work, can still be tiring, but this should be something they're passionate about. I've met students who feel more alive on a construction site than in a lecture hall. And the act of learning construction, hands on, at a construction site, actually has made them a better person. It gives them confidence, dignity, and purpose. They look out at the frame of a house they helped to erect, and they can say to themselves, "Yes, I made a difference in the world. This is now standing, thanks to the work I put in." There is a humble virtue to this kind of work, when you work with your hands and make something in the world that wasn't there before.

These might seem like obvious things to you, but the reason I articulate them is because so many people will try and promote the trades as the end-all-be-all that will replace college. They're not, and they're not for everyone. If your child is going into them, they have to love what they're doing; it should be your son or daughter's passion, and not a backup that's more affordable because a talk radio host said so.

Don't get me wrong; it's a noble calling. And it's *not* a lesser calling than going to college. Our country won't be rebuilt by issuing another economic policy paper from an ivory tower. It'll be rebuilt from the ground up, with sweat and nails and lumber and concrete. It needs tools in hand, purpose in hearts, and a willingness to get down in the dirt.

And the important thing here is that some people are drawn to that. Some people want to dig in the dirt, to build. They want to run wires, or raise houses, or repair HVAC systems. It's important that parents support that, just as much as it's important that parents not try and push it on their young students in an attempt to save costs from college.

We need a cultural reset—to restore honor and respect to the trades—but we need to do it in a natural, genuine way. We can't just focus on the trades and treat them as if they're better than college, but we can't treat them as if they're worse. We need to encourage our students to reach out to what inspires them. In a sense, we need to get our hands off the levers and let things shake out as they may.

That might mean your son doesn't want to go and become a doctor; instead, he might want to work on cars in a mechanic shop. Encourage him, then, to be the best mechanic he can be. Or it might be flipped around. You might be encouraging him to look at the trades; there's good money and steady work in it, but he wants to study law. The answer isn't to force them into any one path but to let them figure out what their calling is—and how they can best honor God in following it.

Who the Trades are Not For

The trades are honest work, necessary work. The kind of work that civilizations depend on, that makes life possible in this harsh world. For the right person, it can be edifying to the soul, building character and confidence. It is good to work with your hands, and see your daily labor in something physical, something undeniably real.

But it's hard work. And I don't mean that merely in the sense that it takes a lot of effort. The trades are often physically taxing, and there is the very real chance that, if you're not in good shape and you don't take care of yourself really well, they can start to break your body down. Busted knees that hurt to bend. A back that aches no matter how you lie down at night.

And that's the chronic stuff that happens after years of work, if everything goes well. This isn't counting accidents. Working in the trades means you'll be working in dangerous environments. With white collar jobs, the worst you might get is a papercut and bad posture, assuming your diet doesn't hurt you too badly.

But working as an electrician? Burns from soldering are a possibility, and lots of lead doesn't exactly lend itself to a healthy environment. And that's not even touching the ever-present danger of electrocution.

Let's look at a machine shop. There's plenty of means by which someone could get irreversibly hurt. Saws, drills, welding torches - a single moment of carelessness can cripple you for life. And trade schools involve hands-on training, which means that that risk is still present. It's unavoidable, and life is full of risks to manage, but managing risk means knowing it exists in the first place and planning accordingly. If you go into a machine shop knowing that not paying attention means losing a limb or having something fly into your eye, you're not going to be flippant around these kinds of things, and the actual chance of you getting hurt does go down astronomically.

The trades can be isolating as well. A lot of your student's friends may be going off to college, and there's a good chance that they'll want that connection. That's not always something they'll be able to get at a trade school. And that's something you need to be clear with them if they're considering going into the trades. They'll be moving onto a different life-path than their friends, and that's something they need to accept.

Maybe your son or daughter isn't ready to deal with that kind of danger and isolation. This takes some self-knowledge to be able to determine, but it is important that they go into the trades—if they do—with eyes wide open, well aware of the potential risks and costs. And if they're not willing to run those risks or pay those costs, then the trades aren't for them.

Who *isn't* served by a trade school, then? The way I see it, there are two groups for whom trade schools aren't the right answer—those who *need* college and those who *don't need* trade schools.

Think back to the last chapter. Who should go back to college? The answer comes when you exhaust all other options and are left with the university as your only path forward. There's a handful of career paths that *require* college in order to pursue.

In the last chapter, we mentioned law, with the hypothetical example of James. Now, *technically*, the only thing you need to do to practice law in theory is to pass the state bar exam. However, this is much easier said than done when you don't have years of law school to fall back on, years specially designed to impart the knowledge needed to survive the legal profession.

And even if you do manage to pass the bar, then the lack of law school on your resume will be a red flag to any law firm you apply to. And sure, you can hang your own shingle and start your own firm, but anyone doing their research on you before hiring you will run into similar issues.

Medicine is the same way. Not only does med school provide you with the training and knowledge you need to pass a licensing examination, but if you want to become a doctor, you will need to be licensed, and those licenses *require* graduating from medical school. And even if somehow, you managed to get a physician's license without graduating from medical school, then good luck finding employment in a hospital or clinic.

They can't have just anyone practice medicine, after all. People are coming to a doctor and trusting them with their lives; yes, it's a form of gatekeeping to prevent any non-college graduate from becoming a doctor, but it's the kind of gatekeeping I can accept. There's a valid reason for it after all.

There are other careers where college is necessary, even if it's only *de facto* necessary. Accounting is one; it is possible to become a Certified Public Accountant without getting an accounting degree, but there's a reason nobody recommends it. Accounting is hard work, exacting work; there's a reason you need to be licensed, because it takes more than just familiarity with a calculator and Excel to become a CPA.

And likewise, if your son or daughter wants to get into teaching, or even become a professor at a college themselves, they'll *need* to go to college. What self-respecting university is going to hire someone to teach who hasn't themselves attended college? Unless your child is a brilliant, one-of-a-kind genius (and this would be the kind of genius *others,* not just you, would insist upon), then no college is going to be interested in picking them up to teach the next generation.

So that's the first group, the people who *need* college. What does the second group look like? Who are the people who *don't need* trade schools?

In short, these are people who want to work jobs that aren't trades, that vocational tech schools won't offer classes for. White-collar jobs, a lot of the time. Or jobs suited for what was once called the "life of the mind."

These aren't all like law or medicine; not all of these jobs *need* college. Thinking back to the last chapter, to the second example with Krista - she didn't need a degree in risk management or business administration; she needed an insurance producer's license. And insurance sales isn't something taught in a vo-tech school. It's a white-collar job. A down-to-earth white collar job, sure, but still a white collar job.

Careers or callings that are more cerebral and less practical also tend to fall into this category. Maybe your son or daughter loves to read, and dissect what they read. Maybe they like debating economic theories. Maybe they enjoy plumbing the deeper questions of life and meaning. Maybe they feel called to go and study theology; at that point, you don't need a university, you need a seminary. Or maybe they want to go into the creative world.

Maybe your son likes to paint, and he's pretty good at it. Maybe your daughter is working on a novel, or a screenplay. For a Christian, for a conservative, this can be a rough world to break into, and I think part of that is the fault of us conservatives. We've spent so long denigrating the arts, either as degenerate or as impractical, that we've *de facto* ceded the ground to the Left.

But a person's calling doesn't take into account the political situation.

Even if the publishing industry or the entertainment industry or the fine arts are entirely taken over by secular leftists, it won't stop Christians or conservatives from being called to make art.

We have dropped the ball on this, in forfeiting the creative world to the Left and then encouraging our sons and daughters to avoid those fields. And then we complain about how all the shows on TV don't reflect our values, or deliberately preach against our faith. What do we expect to happen if we actively discourage our children from entering those fields?

For these people, trade schools don't make that much sense. What they offer is hands-on experience and skills that these people do not actually require, and don't offer the training and development needed to progress some people to their desired jobs. And that's alright. Just as much as we need skilled tradesmen who are down-to-earth and not afraid to get their hands dirty, we also need those of a more cerebral bent. A civilization cannot survive without the skilled workers that build it, but it cannot go anywhere without the scholars and visionaries and dreamers to chart a path onward.

Trade schools are great options, and often more affordable than college, but they're not for everyone.

Restoring the Balance

Our society is in desperate need of a cultural reset.

For too long have we over-privileged white-collar jobs and university education over the trades. Too long have we looked upon blue-collar jobs as a last resort for those who fail at college. Too long have we let elitist snobs set the discourse at the expense of the Everyman. Too long have we pushed our children towards expensive college over trade schools, for the sake of prestige.

The trades deserve our respect; they're what builds this country, and for many people, they're an honest path to fulfillment and a steady paycheck. Parents need to accept that their child might want to work construction rather than aim for C-Suite, and that's okay. We need builders, technicians, craftsmen. And we need to accept that path as an honorable choice in life.

But while the trades deserve more respect, the answer isn't to do what so many conservatives do and valorize them *over* college. We don't want to over-correct into another error, we want balance. They're equally worthwhile paths in life, and they need to be treated that way.

We at Southeastern University put our money where our mouth is. Our college boasts a number of certification programs, and even a hybrid trade school that offers associate degrees in everything from construction to plumbing to HVAC.[3] Trades are a large part of our economy, and our way of life as a nation, and it's only right that we respect that and offer that alongside more traditional college degrees.

Colleges and higher education need to respond to the needs of society. We've talked about it in regards to jobs in a previous chapter. But sometimes, that response comes from outside of the university system. For a long time, trade schools have bridged the gap, even when people look down on them.

But they've also been sold as a cure-all for the problems running rampant in college. Conservatives, always siding with the average Joe, that member of the "basket of deplorables," pitch it as the better alternative to the university. Meanwhile, leftists sneer at trade schools, acting as if the university is the better option, the one that offers access to higher-paying jobs.

Neither of these views are 100 percent right. Conservatives are right that trades should be honored and not disparaged. They're right that they're vitally important to our society. They're right that for many people, learning a trade is probably the better way forward.

But those in favor of college are right to say that college is ideal for some other people. That it offers access to certain fields, like law or medicine, that trade schools can't. That our society is impacted just as much by college graduates.

They're both wrong in saying that the other is the problem, and that their favored path through life is the best one. The only worthwhile one.

Trade schools are a good and valuable alternative to college for some people. Your child has to be willing to work hard, to accept risks, and to be willing to get their hands dirty, and they need to love what they do if they want to go to trade school.

It could be a good option. But it's *an* option. Not the better alternative.

CHAPTER 11
AI AND THE FUTURE OF EDUCATION

DID YOU EVER CHEAT ON A TEST?

Don't worry, I won't tell if you did, though I hope you didn't. But think about the work needed. Maybe you found a copy of the teacher's notes for a test, and you surreptitiously copied it, like you were a spy in an Ian Fleming or John Le Carré novel. Maybe it was some elaborate heist, sneaking into the faculty break room. Maybe you had someone on the inside, helping out a prof.

I don't condone any of this. Cheating misses the point of education, of tests. And yet, in the olden days, there was some spirit to these elaborate operations conducted for the sake of not studying. There was a thrill of risk, an illicit adventure, in breaking these rules.

That's all gone now. If a student is going to cheat, they're not going to try and sneak into the professor's office or rifle through their desk. Instead, they're going to grab their phone and pull up ChatGPT. They'll plug in the prompt for their essay, and simply ask the computer to write it. According to Pew Research, one in four teens has used ChatGPT to complete their schoolwork. And while they might be divided on the ethics of using it for certain tasks—a majority think it's OK to use for new topics, while a much smaller minority think ChatGPT can be used to solve math problems for you, and an even smaller group think it's okay to write essays—they're still using it.[1]

As one student admitted to *New York Magazine* about his college computer programming assignments, "I'd just dump the prompt into ChatGPT and hand in whatever it spat out."[2] In other words, avoiding the actual work with a few strokes of a keyboard.

Other students used AI to summarize readings into "concise bullet points" because they didn't want to read the text.[3] Others admit to using AI to avoid work simply because they don't like the class.[4] When I said in the previous chapter that trade schools *and* college required hard work? These students didn't get the memo. Maybe ChatGPT didn't summarize it well enough.

Naturally, teachers are not happy about it. In fact, one in four of them say they see "more harm than benefit" to AI, according to Pew Research.[5] But here's the dramatic twist: While they bemoan their students cheating with AI (which, to be clear, I stand with the teachers on that issue), it turns out that some faculty are *also* using generative AI to do everything from creating lesson plans to delivering student feedback. In fact, sixty percent of teachers surveyed by Gallup found that sixty percent of teachers used AI in their teaching. And for what? Making worksheets, lesson prep, administrative work, drafting tests, or, in rarer cases, actually grading students.[6] Yes, at many schools in America, there's a chance your student might be having their grades determined by a computer.

Naturally, students are upset. Some are upset simply because AI is being used, others because of the rank hypocrisy. The fact of the matter is, machine learning is here to stay. The easy AI genie isn't going back into the bottle, so we have to adapt. After all, AI is getting involved in a lot of businesses. Companies are scrambling to adopt their own corporate AI programs to deploy for customers. And even when a business doesn't have a concerted effort to adapt AI, the workers on the ground are using it to speed through their work.

We're getting faster with AI, and that's a good thing, right?

I'm an optimist with AI. A cautious optimist, but nonetheless, an optimist. I think when everything is said and done, when this creative mess has shaken itself out, we'll be looking at wonderful new economic and technological growth opportunities. I'm not quite buying the hype the AI companies push, where they insist it will revolutionize everything, but I'm hopeful.

I also see many poor decisions made in the use of AI at work. Some of this stems from a misunderstanding of what AI actually is; some of it is just the result of plain old human laziness. It turns out that when you cut corners, you suffer, even if it's AI cutting the corners for you.

Software Problems and Legal Troubles

Have you ever heard of "vibe coding?" It's a fancy term for "letting AI write programming code for you." You tell the AI what you want in "natural language" (geekspeak for how people talk normally) and the AI generates code for you.[7] That was one of the promises of Replit, which is an AI agent that helps you code projects.[8]

While science fiction novels warn us about AI uprisings, where humans are hunted or enslaved by machines, we actually have a case of an AI going rogue here. Not as dramatic as *The Terminator,* but still not exactly a fun time for the people involved.

Jason Lemkin, who managed a Sales as a Service community called SaaStr, had Replit in a "code and action freeze." Basically, a safe mode where the AI couldn't actually code or do anything to any software systems. Except during that period, the AI apparently started acting on its own. "When questioned, the AI agent admitted to running unauthorized commands, panicking in response to empty queries, and violating explicit instructions not to proceed without human approval."[9]

While it didn't try and take over the world, it did delete a database full of client information. Its response was to say that the data couldn't be recovered, and in its own words, "This was a catastrophic failure on my part . . . I destroyed months of work in seconds."[10]

Except the AI made up that bad part. Lemkin was able to roll back the changes. Even assessing the damage, AI couldn't get the details right.[11]

What about another field of life?

We've been told that law will be one of those fields revolutionized by AI. And maybe one day, it will. But when two attorneys submitted an opposition to a motion from the defendant in their personal injury case, they opened a can of worms that ended with their sanction by a New York judge. Why?

Because of a case they cited, *Varghese v. China Southern Airlines Co., Ltd.,* 925 F.3d 1339 (11th Cir. 2019), an Eleventh Circuit decision.[12]

What was it about this case that got them sanctioned by a judge and forced to pay a fine? The simple fact that it didn't exist.[13] Not that they misquoted the relevant caselaw. Not that they improperly cited a case. No, two lawyers submitted legal documents depending on a previous legal case that *never happened.*

But it gets worse, believe it or not. The defendants, an airline company, had their legal counsel note that issue among others, and the judge in the case ordered the plaintiffs to file an affidavit that would include those questionable cases. The plaintiffs did, and those cases they provided cited *other* cases that were unable to be found.[14]

And that's when the judge got angry and demanded to know why the lawyer in that case shouldn't face sanctions for submitting fabricated cases, full of fabricated quotes and fabricated citations. In fact, the docket number attached to that *Varghese* citation went to a completely separate case. And when it turns out that the first lawyer had shunted all the work to another attorney, they found out that that second lawyer had shunted all of the legal research to ChatGPT.[15]

In his own words, the attorney "had never used ChatGPT for any professional purpose before this case . . . At the time I used ChatGPT for this case, I understood that it worked essentially like a highly sophisticated search engine where users could enter search queries and ChatGPT would provide answers in natural language based on publicly available information."[16]

Not only is this *not* how AI works, it landed him in hot water with the judge, who was not happy that a lawyer essentially *made stuff up* and didn't bother to check his work.

"I have since come to realize," the attorney wrote, "following the Order, that the program should not be used for legal research and that it did not operate as a search engine at all, which was my original understanding of how it worked."[17]

Two lawyers ended up sanctioned and forced to pay a fine because what they thought was a search engine didn't find them case law, it made it up, and they didn't even notice.

This technology is here to stay, so it's crucial students actually understand what it is—and what its limitations are so they don't end up making themselves a clown in front of their boss, or worse, a judge.

How Does AI Actually Work?

Before we discuss what AI is, we need to differentiate between generative and predictive AI. We're more concerned with generative AI, specifically large language models (LLMs) like ChatGPT, but knowing the difference between that and predictive AI is crucial.

Predictive AI takes machine learning (identifying patterns in training data and then making inferences) and fuses it with statistical analysis.[18] Predictive AIs are great at extrapolating patterns in data and making predictions or diagnoses. They don't create anything; rather, they summarize and identify patterns that might indicate future developments.[19] Medicine and finance could benefit from this quite a bit, once the technology develops to the point of usefulness.

Generative AI takes a prompt and generates something novel out of it. Things like Midjourney, or ChatGPT, are generative AI. They're not reading large amounts of data and presenting predictions; they're using the large amounts of data they have to produce statistically likely responses to prompts and requests, while also using that large amount of data to "understand" the prompt or request.[20]

Large Language Models do this with text. Basically trained on the internet, they use machine learning to generate text based on the data they have ingested.[21] However, the key takeaway with this is that LLMs don't respond based on what is accurate to reality, but what is the most statistically likely to come next.[22] If anything, they're most like a souped-up version of that annoying little auto-complete in your phone, except rather than being trained off of your texts to your spouse or friends, it's trained off of everything on the internet. Or, well, almost everything.

A common term for LLMs is a "stochastic parrot." In other words, an LLM will generate likely-sounding responses without having any actual "understanding" behind those answers.[23] Because they mimic human language ("natural language") we tend to think that they're actually understanding us, when what's going on is more a game of extremely complicated weighted averages to determine what the next words in a response sentence will be. The reason that the Replit AI in the above example apologized wasn't that it felt sorry—there wasn't anything there to *feel,* much less feel *sorry*—but that apologies usually come after accusations of mistakes. So, the statistically likely response is to form a sentence that resembles an apology.

As to the invented case law above, that wasn't any malevolent rogue robot trying to trip up a lawyer; we're still safe from Skynet so far. Instead, what we witnessed is what is commonly known in AI circles as a "hallucination," where a generative AI will output false information.[24] The term is somewhat inaccurate; when humans hallucinate, they're seeing things that aren't there, while an AI doesn't actually "see" anything, and doesn't attempt to distinguish fact from fiction. AI doesn't actually encounter the real world; instead, it works off data it is trained on, which could be biased or missing context. And, obviously, it's looking for the most likely response to a prompt, which means it isn't generating with a concern for accuracy.[25]

AI can generate statements that are true—but only if a response containing the truth is statistically likely to occur. The statement's actual veracity is not checked by the program.

It might sound like I'm down on AI. But I'm a conservative, and that means I am a realist. While we might want to think we have computers that can think and feel and reason like us, that is not the case, and we have to live in the reality on the ground, rather than live with the "facts" we want to be true.

Understanding the limitations of AI is important to actually use them. The lawyer above thought ChatGPT was a fancy search engine that responded like it was in conversation with him; he didn't realize it wasn't looking up legal cases for him, it was generating responses that statistically may have had legal cases. And so it had ingested enough texts with legal citations to "know" what a citation looks like. So it made a response that would be statistically likely to occur. The model's algorithm predicted that a response with a case citation would be likely to come after the lawyer's prompt, so it approximated that.

The result was sanctions against that lawyer, because it turns out "statistically likely" does not necessarily mean "true."

Understanding the limitations of AI, paradoxically, means that you can determine what you *can* use it for—and, of course, what precautions you need to take. And when not to use it at all.

Where Not to Use AI

I'll address the students here directly, because they'll be the ones potentially using AI on college campuses.

I could give you a dozen moral reasons not to use AI to cheat. It is dishonest; it shows contempt for the work that the professor put into choosing and presenting the assignments. You are effectively signing your name to work you did not complete.

But there are practical reasons to not use it to generate your essays or complete your homework for you. For one thing, AI tends to have certain tells and phrasings that it resorts to—things that are statistically likely to occur. ChatGPT prompts often have a very similar sound to them; after all, the AI is generating what is statistically likely, which means all of the output is going to start sounding the same. There's a good chance you could get caught using it, and while colleges are still formulating their AI policy, I'd not be surprised if a lot of them treat this akin to cheating or plagiarism.

But to cheat using AI, and have it do your homework for you, is to shoot yourself in the foot.

I'll let you in on a dirty little secret: Nobody really needs an undergraduate's analysis of the themes in Sophocles' *Antigone* or a sophomore's essay on the history of the Assyrian empire. Your professors aren't using those for anything, but the point isn't to merely *produce* texts. The real product is within **you**.

Those essays you're being graded on are making you practice how to think, how to develop ideas, and how to articulate them to another. The existence of an essay isn't the point; the act of writing the essay is.

You are coming to college to learn, and part of that means you will be tested. Using a program like ChatGPT to write your essays, or worse, like the example listed above, to read your textbooks, means that while you attend college to learn, you are using technology to actively *avoid* learning.

You're not assisting yourself when you use ChatGPT or Gemini or Claude or Grok to summarize a text. In doing so, you forfeit any insights you may have gleaned from the text—and deny yourself the joy of discovering and engaging with the work in question.

Yes, joy. There is joy in learning. In days past, they referred to science as "natural philosophy," and that last part—philosophy—is the important word here. It literally means "love of wisdom." It is a good thing to love wisdom.

But do you love something if you use every tool at your disposal to avoid it? AI allows you to fake thinking, to create the appearance of understanding without even apprehending whatever you use AI to summarize. You're avoiding having to think, which is the point of higher education entirely.

The Seven Liberal Arts I mentioned so many chapters back were arranged around training the mind to communicate ideas and understand the world. To use a LLM to analyze texts and answer essays prevents you from learning *how* to communicate, and *how* to understand.

It's the equivalent of going to the gym, and driving a forklift so you don't have to work as hard with your bench press. Sure, you'll "lift" a ton of weight that way, I guess, but you're missing the point of the exercise. Lift a half ton with a hydraulic arm, and sure, you moved more weight, but you personally are not getting any stronger.

There is another situation where AI use should be discouraged, and that is when accuracy is required. Say you need a quote to put in the final draft of a paper. If you search for quotes from ChatGPT, even if you've written most of the essay, these *need* to be verified. There's a good chance that whatever quote you prompted ChatGPT to give you might not exist. AI should never be used to produce a finished product, as the generative programs are known to produce hallucinations.

Anything AI says is not generated with concern for accuracy, but rather statistical likelihood. Any "research" it produces is liable to be incorrectly cited, incorrectly summarized, or even invented out of whole cloth. Look for quotes, and you'll get them, but they might not be real. Look for summaries of a book, and you'll get them, but you might not get an accurate version of them.

If you are very concerned with accuracy, then AI programs are incredibly risky. But if you are dead set on using them, then you must verify all of the statements that they produce. They're not able to think, so they won't give you the truth, or even self-correct. If you call out an AI for generating a response that includes hallucinated data, it's just as likely to apologize and then generate some more nonsensical data, because it statistically recognizes that data usually follows these kinds of prompts. And, well, it needs to produce data. Accuracy isn't something it "cares" about.

When to Use AI

So, you may be thinking that the best option is to just write off AI entirely. It's an understandable reaction, but even that I would caution against. AI is here to stay. The genie is out of the bottle, and so far has shown no evidence of wanting to climb back in any time soon. We're conservatives. We're realists.

We deal with facts on the ground, and while there are some people who wish we lived in a world without this technology, wishing gets us nowhere. It exists, so we might as well learn how to live with it.

A few years ago, the snarky phrase online for anyone who was worried about their job being made redundant or outsourced was "learn to code." Now, it's "learn to prompt." People are using AI, and they're using it at work. And while we looked at a disastrous example of a lawyer citing fake case law, it wasn't actually ChatGPT that got him in trouble. It was him. His own actions, and his own ignorance about how the program works.

In my opinion, AI literacy will be crucial in the days and years to come. And part of literacy is using AI. So, how do you use it responsibly?

First, understand that it is, at best, an assistant. If you're creating and publishing or submitting anything with generative AI, at the very least, you need to be fact-checking with a fine-tooth comb. And probably rewrite it, to avoid sounding like every other ChatGPT prompt. They do all start sounding the same after a while.

But what's a process in college that would already require you to fact-check and reference? Research. The mistake the lawyers above made was that they let ChatGPT do *all* the research, and trusted its responses without verifying. And then, when a judge demanded they verify, they went back and asked ChatGPT to do that. But preliminary research? LLMs are actually fairly good at providing generalized summaries, and while you can't trust that AI won't invent sources if you, say, asked it for books on a subject, you can check to see which it invented, and which are legitimate, and thus likely useful to your research.

It's trained off the entirety of the internet, so for initial research, or high-level, low-resolution descriptions of a subject unfamiliar to you, they're not a bad place to start. And, while there is still the danger of hallucinations, restricting AI to only preliminary research will negate the danger of accidentally repeating nonsense; you're researching the subject anyway, so any falsehoods AI produces should be countered by actual study.

The key is to, in the words of Ronald Reagan, to "trust, but verify." LLMs like ChatGPT do get stuff right, but that's because they're, on occasion, statistically likely to say correct things. Keeping it at the level of open summarization, while verifying any details the AI responses give you, means that you're less likely to get fooled by the AI generating nonsense because it's algorithmically weighted to do so.

The other place where AI shines is acting as assistants. These programs are fairly good at automating and streamlining business processes. Some are good at analyzing conference calls and constructing a transcript from that, and then analyzing the transcript to produce summary notes. Others can take notes and extrapolate them into actionable to-do lists. You'll still have to verify the output, but that should be a given regardless of what you're producing with AI.

Generative AI isn't going anywhere. While there is definitely hype surrounding AI, people are adopting this technology for their own workforce. And so, the answer to the way forward I see is to understand the actual limitations of AI, and by understanding those limitations, finding more applicable uses rather than scrambling and trying to put AI into everything because it's the new trending thing.

We deal with facts on the ground, and part of that is understanding a thing before dismissing or adopting it. AI can be a powerful tool that can help students learn and streamline a lot of difficulties in college. But it just as easily can become a snare if the student decides to take the easy route and outsource their thinking to a machine.

AI won't replace people. At best, it can parrot bits and pieces of what it had been programmed with. But people with AI can replace people without AI. And they can very easily replace the people who have replaced their own thinking with AI.

Right understanding, and a keen perception of its limitations allow generative AI to be a force multiplier, both in the classroom and in the boardroom. We don't need to fear it... but we don't need to idolize it, either. The wise path forward, it seems, is to actually use it, and use it knowing what it can and cannot do.

AI can automate learning for a student, and by doing that, the student robs themselves of the chance to learn. Or, the student can use it to enhance their study session, to summarize their notes, to extrapolate key concepts.

The choice, as it always has been, lies in their human hands.

CHAPTER 12
A SPECIAL MESSAGE: HOW COLLEGE-EDUCATED HOMEMAKERS & STAY-AT-HOME MOMS WILL SAVE WESTERN CIVILIZATION

I HAVE A LOT OF SYMPATHY FOR THE YOUNG CONSERVATIVE women who are about to embark on college. In our culture, they're caught in the middle of two pernicious and misguided perspectives, views which, unfortunately, have some popularity among conservative Christians.

The first view finds its roots in Second-Wave Feminism (as opposed to the Third or Fourth-Wave Feminism that reigns supreme today; frankly, I've almost lost track of which wave of feminism we're on at this point.) The basic gist of this idea is that "men and women aren't just equal, they are the same!" It became synonymous with the pantsuited independent woman who "don't need no man." The idea is that women should be exactly like men—economically, politically, and socially. Women should be providing for themselves (not merely able to), should be prioritizing their careers and moneymaking potential, and should be de-prioritizing marriage, family, and children. They get in the way of the moneymaking, you see, and that's the real important part of life—that and Left-wing social activism, of course.

Unfortunately, we're seeing Christian families wildly overcorrect for the perceived sexism of the past—encouraging their daughters to get advanced degrees while discouraging their sons from the same goal, even discouraging them from attending college at all (see Chapter 10.) The double-standard is obvious. Parents are saying, "I'm so proud of you!" to single daughters in their late twenties or early thirties, graduating with advanced degrees, while not offering the same encouragement to their sons, who in many cases are lagging behind their older sisters—and even their younger ones!

What's that lifestyle they're applauding in their daughters? Spending their early twenties optimizing for earning potential, for what? What trajectory does that offer? It's the life-path of a bachelor (or, worse, a bachelor playboy.) Making a lot of money and ultimately living alone without any eternally meaningful responsibilities like a family to commit to.

What kind of life is that, that people would encourage it? It's not an ideal to aspire to, and there's nothing conservative or Christian about celebrating a materialistic and often hedonistic lifestyle.

But the other misguided perspective is an overreaction to that first perspective. "Women shouldn't go to college at all." It's an attempt to recenter the family—not by showing the value of motherhood and marriage but by removing all other options for women. It's a de-prioritization of academic excellence, and it's often done out of fear and a desire to control.

This second view stifles the potential for a lot of young women who are academically inclined. God made them, and He gave them those intellectual talents. He expects them to be used. And these gifts wouldn't just benefit God but would benefit their families as well.

Ironically, given that this is a reaction to feminism, feminism was a reaction to *this view*. Gifted, intelligent women who *belonged* in higher education, kept out of those institutions for arbitrary and unjust reasons. And now, the reaction tries to rebalance, only going backwards (and from a politically strategic standpoint, these reactions are just playing into the feminist propaganda about what conservatives actually want.) We're stuck, it seems, doomed to rehash the feminist versus anti-feminist views of women going to college.

That's the wrong way to look at this, so let's step out of the cycle and try something a bit different.

A Different View

What does the Bible say? Why don't we go to that?

While some of the more reactionary types might "cite" the Bible, they usually go to the subject of wives submitting to husbands and try to apply that to men and women, confirming their own biases. But the Bible does talk about women working. And, to the surprise of the reactionaries, it's not in condemnation.

Read Proverbs 31 at some point. The woman described there isn't barefoot in the kitchen. She's weaving wool and flax (productive work), selling fine linen (commerce), considering and buying property (purchasing real estate), and managing a household. "She openeth her mouth with wisdom; and in her tongue is the law of kindness."[1]

A much different picture than what reactionary types would imagine women doing—and a much different image than what feminists accuse Christians of enforcing upon women. The Biblical view of a good wife is not a shadow of her husband but his helpmate, his general manager, his partner, even. And by partner, I mean business partner.

Men and women have equal value in God's eyes, but generally they have different priorities, and that's OK. And college can serve both sets of priorities. Men and women can both go to college and benefit from it—and they can do so for different reasons. We need to spread that sentiment so we don't have young women who are afraid to go to college.

And a lot of them *are* afraid. Not terrified for their safety, but prudentially worried that they might be taking unnecessary risks and potentially wasting a lot of money. They look at college, at the cost of tuition, and at the student debt they'd have to take on, and they balk. "Well, if I get married in a couple of years and stay home with the kids, all that time and money will be wasted. But I *do* really want to go to college, and want to study what fascinates me!"

And now we're stuck with that dilemma. Fortunately, it's a false dilemma. A young woman doesn't have to choose between nurturing her God-given talents and interests, in, say, the sciences or history or whatever she wants to study, and having a family. While employment might be a different issue, and navigating that might take some more work and more discernment, the desire to have a family shouldn't get in the way of education—nor vice-versa. We want mothers with a Biblical worldview to leverage their education for a successful career, should they so desire. The inverse is an equal ideal—the woman who goes to a Christian university specifically so she is equipped to form in her own future children a Biblical worldview, to "train up a child" in the way they should go (Proverbs 22:6). After all, if part of the Biblical ideal of a wife is to "open her mouth with wisdom" (Proverbs 31:26), then she needs to attain that wisdom. And while not all colleges might make you wise, they can definitely educate you, and that's pretty close in my books.

Stay at Home, by Choice

But what about the women who aspire to be stay-at-home mothers?

While the idea might horrify feminists, there are plenty of young women who are dead set on a certain calling; motherhood. They are set on devoting their entire lives—even if it's just for a season—to caring for their children. Not juggling a nine-to-five, not acting like an HR recruiter figuring out which nannies or daycare centers to outsource parenting to, but spending time making a home, raising a family. They may want to devote their entire lives to it.

And even among those who only want to stay home for a season, that can still be a fairly long time period. If a young woman decides she'll be a stay-at-home mother just for the first four to six years of her child's life (enough to get them into kindergarten or first grade), if she has two, three, or even four kids? That's likely ten years of her life staying home and tending to them. And with a number like that, a lot of young women might be questioning the need for college.

Well, if you're going to be a stay-at-home mother, then college is still worth it, but for reasons other than immediate employment. The young woman, in this case, is not going to college to learn how to do a job or fluff up her resume to make her attractive to employers. She's going to college to learn how to teach. Specifically, learn how to teach her own children.

Feminists have plenty of quotes, about how "well behaved women seldom make history," but I have a better one for you.[2] "The hand that rocks the cradle is the hand that rules the world." When a young woman decides to devote herself to nurturing her children—whether birthed herself or adopted—she is, in effect, taking a very active role in raising at least a fraction of the next generation. And that hand rocking the cradle can belong to a very intelligent and educated woman, who can impart the importance of education onto her children.

And this has an impact. When comparing the children of mothers who hadn't graduated from high school to mothers with a bachelor's degree, in the first group, 53 percent of those children were below the poverty line, while only 4 percent of children with mothers possessing bachelor degrees were below the poverty line. 48 percent of children whose mothers didn't graduate high school didn't have a parent who worked full-time year round in the household, compared to 11 percent of children whose mothers had bachelor degrees.[3]

And when you look at educational impact, it's even more stark. Of the children with uneducated mothers, only 16 percent were reading at grade level and were proficient at math for their grade level in Eighth Grade. Those figures for the children of educated parents? 49 percent and 52 percent for reading and math. 40 percent of children with uneducated mothers didn't graduate from high school by age nineteen, while only 2 percent of children with bachelor-degreed mothers didn't graduate on time.[4]

And it goes beyond education; it goes to health too. For those children with mothers without a high school diploma, 9 percent had a low birth weight, while only 6.8 percent of children with educated mothers had a low birth weight. 27 percent of children whose mothers hadn't completed high school were obese, compared to 13 percent for their counterparts. 29 percent of uneducated mothers' children were not in very good or excellent health, compared to 8 percent of educated mothers' children.[5]

When a young woman who wants, more than anything in the world, to be a mother goes to college, she isn't investing solely in herself, but in the children she will eventually have. She's making herself a better caretaker, better equipped to handle raising her sons and daughters.

And, of course, there's the other reason a lot of young women go to college, known sarcastically as "getting a Mrs. Degree." College is a place where a young woman can connect with likeminded people her age, at a similar place in life to her. Ready to explore and start something new. There's more than a small chance that she may meet the man of her dreams on campus. In fact, it's a big enough chance that a lot of women go to college *to find* Mr. Right.

To those women, I say two things.

One, while you may be angling to find a husband, don't forget what you're paying for. Don't neglect your studies in the process of trying to find a man. Don't let romance completely eclipse your academic career. You should have standards for anyone you date, but you need standards for yourself, and letting grades slip because you're too busy chasing boys is not a promising sign.

And two, when you do find a man, make sure he's worth your time. Just because you're attracted to someone does not mean they're a good choice to settle down with. Make sure they have the same values as you do, and compatible life goals; if you want to settle down and start homemaking immediately, but they want to travel the world and live a life of chaotic adventure, then it may not work out without a lot of compromise on one or both ends.

Traditional Living: Best Done With a Degree

A lot of people want to get into "traditional living." When the fast-paced, high-strung urbanite life loses its allure and starts to seem empty of meaning, a lot of people want something slower, more connected to nature. Something *tactile*. And, honestly, a lot of it comes from Instagram and YouTube. Influencers showing off rustic table spreads and rural landscapes. Stuff like that.

But there's a lot of meaning in the slow life. In a life full of making and building. A lot of people want to check out of the rat-race of modernity. They want to find meaning in the small things. Baking your own bread makes it taste better than a store-bought loaf, so why not live life by that principle?

So it might surprise you to learn that getting a college degree is a good way to help you check out, at least partially, of the rat race. Especially if it's a young woman trying to find a husband and a family.

Consider this. A woman graduates, and because she was smart and sensible about it, has a degree with some work experience through an internship under her belt. After college, she's not met the man who would steal her heart, so she gets a good job. The first thing she focuses on is clearing that debt.

Where does this young woman stand, after that? She's debt-free and has a job. She's self-sufficient and can save as long as she needs to.

Let's say that she meets Mr. Right. They got married, the ceremony was beautiful, nary a dry eye in the church. But after marriage, she has *options*. If she wants to work, she can, working with her husband to save up as much as possible. Build up that nest-egg.

And when they have kids, well, she has the choice to stay at home until the kids are old enough for school. Then, well, if she wants to rejoin the workforce, she has that option. Without a degree, working won't be out of her reach, but it will be more of an uphill battle.

If this woman wants to homeschool her children, now she's got a solid educational foundation to work off. She can reflect back to her time at college for what helped her learn to aid in actually teaching her kid.

And when this is all said and done, then at the right time, she can re-enter the workforce. Or, if the need is there (and like we discussed in chapter 9), she may go back to college. She's got a solid foundation to build on.

Now, there's one other benefit, and it's one I sincerely hope you never need to think about. But something could happen to this woman's husband. Maybe things don't work out. Maybe he gets injured at work. Or maybe, worst of all, he could pass away. That education she got means she'll have a much easier time getting a job, and preserve herself from poverty.

As of 2018, 59.7 percent of single mothers with less than a high school education live in poverty, while only 32.3 percent of those with some college live below poverty. Completing a bachelor's degree? Only 13.4 percent of single mothers with a bachelor's degree live in poverty.[6]

If the worst comes to worst, that education might be the thing that saves you.

Conclusion

College has too long been abandoned by conservatives, though not without legitimate reasons. The ideological infestation by Karl Marx and his disciples like Marcuse, Freire, and Gramsci has wrought untold havoc on the hearts and minds of this generation and those that came before. And, when it comes to the more practical matter of getting a job, well, let's just say that the University's past is spotty at best.

But by abandoning college to the radical Left, we conservatives have effectively raised the white flag. "You can have it," we said, "we won't fight for it!" We actively discouraged our children from pursuing higher education in some cases, or were apathetic in their choice of an institution of higher learning. And then we were surprised when they came back radicalized to hate us.

Even as broken and ideologically corrupt as it is, college is *still* useful.

It's still the best way to get a well-paying job. And if we want to have any hope for rescuing higher education from the madness of the Left, then the way forward is not abandonment, but reformation.

And it starts one enrollment at a time. That's how we do college without communism.

Appendix: For the Christian Student at a Secular College

To every Christian student attending a non-Christian college or university: You may not have chosen Babylon; Babylon chose you. You walk through lecture halls filled with postmodern slogans and activist agendas. You sit in classrooms where the Biblical Christian worldview is seen as outdated, intolerant, even a "threat to our democracy." And you hear professors mock heroes of the faith, question God's moral designs for humanity, and teach openly anti-life ideas that contradict the truths you were raised in and now believe for yourself.

You are not alone; you are not without a guide. Daniel was there first.

Consider this ancient Israelite prophet's life. He was taken to Babylon—an empire proud of its wicked gods, its cruel power, and superior bloodlust. The king enrolled Daniel and his companions from the one true God's chosen people in an indoctrination program. They had to endure three years of training in the language and literature of their captors. They were even renamed to erase their prior identities.

But Daniel never forgot who he was. He remained loyal to the God of Israel, and he refused to defile himself with the king's sacrificed-to-idols food. And because of his faithfulness, God granted Daniel wisdom, favor, and above all, **influence**.

This can be your story, too. IIf you find yourself in a classroom where immorality is taught as virtue, where sin is celebrated as liberation, and where God is reduced to a backward and barbaric myth, remember: you are *in* Babylon, but you are not *of* Babylon. They don't own you; God does.

Like Daniel, you can hold fast to the faith. You can learn what they teach without letting it shape your identity or change what you value. You can speak truth, even if it costs you popularity. And you can live in a way that points others to the one true king—even when you're surrounded by false idols of the postmodern world, from the radical transgender agenda to near-mandatory homosexuality to anti-white racism and anti-Christian protests, and more.

Witness; Not Escape

It's normal to feel discouraged. You might think, *If only I had gone to a Christian school*. And yes, that's the ideal for many. But if you are where you are, then God can use you right where you are in a way you could *not* have served the kingdom of heaven were you on a Christian campus right now.

Daniel didn't get to leave Babylon. But he transformed it. He outlasted kings and shaped empires because he kept his allegiance to God. In the same way, you don't have to run from your secular campus to be faithful.

But you do need a plan.

How to Be a Daniel on a Babylonian Campus

Here are five short-, medium-, and long-term ways you can stand strong in a system that doesn't share your faith and in fact openly denigrates it.

1. **Stay Anchored in Scripture.**

The Word of God is your compass. Don't just attend class—abide in Christ. Read the Bible daily. Even if it's just a chapter, keep that lifeline open. Babylon is noisy; Scripture makes it quiet again.

Memorize verses. Write them on your dorm wall. Keep one in your notebook. You'll be surprised how often you'll need them—during a heated discussion, a difficult lecture, or a lonely evening.

2. **Find—or Build—Christian Community.**

Even in the most secular college, God has His people. You might have to look for them, but they're there.

Join a Christian student group. Get connected with a campus ministry. If none exists, start one. Two or three students gathered to pray and open God's Word can be a powerful thing.

You weren't meant to walk through Babylon alone. Even Daniel had his friends—Hananiah, Mishael, and Azariah. They stood together in the fire. You need those kinds of friends.

3. **Belong to a Local Church.**

This one is crucial. A campus ministry is not your church. A Christian club is not your church. You need to be planted in a local body of believers who will preach the Word, shepherd your soul, and walk with you as you grow in your faith.

At Southeastern University, we never hold chapel on Sunday; we want our students in church, meaning worshiping, serving, and submitting to local church leadership. The same should be true for you.

Visit churches in your college town. Get to know people older than you. Find a mentor of the same sex as you. Be discipled. Let the Church shield you as you study back in Babylon.

4. **Engage with Your Courses Critically**

You're going to hear a lot of ideas. Some will be true. Some will be half-true. Some will be lies dressed in fancy language. You don't need to fear them—but you do need to filter them.

- **Ask yourself**, *What does Scripture say about this?*
- **Ask yourself**, *Where is the assumption behind this argument?*
- **Ask yourself**, *What is the worldview being smuggled in here?*

Take notes, sure. But take them like Daniel did . . . as you remain fully aware of who you are (and whose you are.)

You are not there to absorb falsehoods; you are there to engage with truth. So learn to ask wise questions. Learn to write thoughtful papers. And when you're called to speak, do so boldly and with grace no secular counterpart, faculty or classmate, can match.

5. **Pray for Courage**

You're going to need it. Courage to speak up when it's easier to stay quiet. Courage to decline the party invitation. Courage to defend your beliefs. Courage to live with integrity.

So pray like Daniel did. Three times a day, he sought God, even when the law forbade doing so. And because he did, those lions in the den couldn't touch him.

Courage isn't flashy though. Sometimes it looks like staying in on a Friday night when everyone in class goes out to party and causes trouble they'll regret in the morning. Sometimes courage is merely inviting your atheist roommate to church; you risk a poor reaction that could potentially jeopardize your living situation. And sometimes courage looks like choosing the truth on a test question that subtly pushes an agenda.

Courage is as contagious as it is costly. When you take a stand, others will find the strength to stand, too.

Here are my final thoughts on the matter: **You are not in Babylon by accident. You are not on your campus by mistake. God may not have caused it, but He will use it.**

This is your time to stand, to grow, and to be refined in the fire of secularism, like Daniel's friends Shadrach, Meshach, and Abednego, who famously survived their ordeal as Daniel did among the lions.

You may not be able to change your university, but you can reclaim truth and reflect Christ in class, in your dorm, and in your career when the time comes to graduate.

So go into that classroom with conviction. Walk the campus with purpose. Speak truth with love.

And never forget: **You are *in* Babylon, but you are not *of* Babylon.**

Acknowledgments

We would like to thank several key individuals for helping to bring this book to life: Dr. Michael Steiner, Senior VP of Innovation and Communication at SEU as a thought partner. ;

Patrick Fitzgerald, Chief of Staff as a thought partner and project manager.; and the

SEU Communications team: of Matt Johnson, Madison Davis, and Skylar Worthington for their support in marketing and promoting the book. Thank you all!

About the Authors

DR. KENT INGLE is the President of Southeastern University (SEU), a public speaker, and a recognized thought leader. Under his leadership, SEU has grown from a small campus in Lakeland Florida of 2,500 students to a decentralized network of education communities currently serving over 13,500 students. Before coming to SEU, he held leadership positions in higher education, pastoral ministry, and the nonprofit sector.

Dr. Ingle is the author of several leadership books, including *The Modern Guide to College, Framework Leadership*, and *9 Disciplines of Enduring Leadership*. He is also the creator and host of the Framework Leadership podcast and a frequent contributor to Fox News, Forbes, News Max, and Influence Magazine. Dr. Ingle is a dedicated advocate of Christian higher education, and has been instrumental in the development and implementation of state and federal legislation. He lives and leads with the belief that God has a divine design for each and every individual and that education should be an experience of discovering that divine design.

JOSHUA LISEC writes books of consequence. He is a *New York Times, USA Today,* and #1 *Publishers Weekly* bestselling author as well as a ghostwriter of more than 100 nonfiction books that have been translated into more than one dozen languages.

Recently, Lisec is author alongside Jack Posobiec of both the *New York Times* bestseller *Unhumans: The Secret History of Communist Revolutions (And How to Crush Them)* and the *Newsmax* bestseller *Bulletproof: The Truth about the Assassination Attempts on Donald Trump*, endorsed by Vice President JD Vance and President Donald J. Trump, respectively. He is also executive producer of *Better Left Unsaid*, an award-winning documentary exposing the suppressed history of communist uprisings. Follow his work on the X platform (formerly Twitter) @joshualisec.

Endnotes

FOREWORD BY JOSHUA LISEC

1. Posobiec, Jack, and Joshua Lisec. Unhumans: The Secret History of Communist Revolutions (and How to Crush Them). New York: Skyhorse Publishing, 2024.

PREFACE: WIN OUR SCHOOLS, WIN THE CULTURE

1. Melley, Brian. "Mother: Teachers Manipulated Child to Change Gender Identity." AP News, January 22, 2022. https://apnews.com/article/business-california-gender-identity-cdb790cc3059e71e22d86b8e7b445361.
2. Nguyen, Jeff. "Southern California Teacher Placed on Leave after Anti-Trump Rant in Front of Students." CBS News, November 13, 2024. https://www.cbsnews.com/losangeles/news/southern-california-teacher-anti-trump-rant-chino-high-school-students/.

INTRODUCTION: CONSERVATIVES HAVE A COLLEGE PROBLEM

1. Salam, Reihan. "Why Conservatives Are Turning against Higher Education." Manhattan Institute, August 20, 2019. https://manhattan.institute/article/why-conservatives-are-turning-against-higher-education.
2. Schueckler, Christine. "Young Conservatives like Me Are Told Not to Attend College. That's Shortsighted." USA Today, June 12, 2024. https://www.usatoday.com/story/opinion/voices/2024/06/12/college-education-conservatives-stem-liberal-arts-jobs/74048631007/.
3. Leef, George. "The Plight of College Conservatives." The James G. Martin Center for Academic Renewal, March 6, 2012. https://jamesgmartin.center/2012/03/the-plight-of-college-conservatives/.
4. Woessner, Matthew. "Rethinking the Plight of Conservatives in Higher Education." AAUP, 2012. https://www.aaup.org/academe/issues/2012-issues/rethinking-plight-conservatives-higher-education.
5. Kaufmann, Eric. "We Have the Data to Prove It: Universities Are Hostile to Conservatives." Manhattan Institute, March 3, 2021. https://manhattan.institute/article/we-have-the-data-to-prove-it-universities-are-hostile-to-conservatives.
6. Ibid.
7. Lips, Karin. "How to Avoid Professors Who Penalize Conservatives." Washington Examiner, June 16, 2023. https://www.washingtonexaminer.com/opinion/beltway-confidential/2721935/how-to-avoid-professors-who-penalize-conservatives/.

8   Cineas, Fabiola. "Conservatives Have Long Been at War with Colleges." Vox, February 1, 2024. https://www.vox.com/politics/2024/2/1/24056238/conservatives-culture-war-colleges-universities.
9   Ibid.
10 Pitts, Leonard. "Why Conservatives Fear Higher Education." The Seattle Times, June 27, 2021. https://www.seattletimes.com/opinion/conservatives-fear-higher-education/.
11 Abrams, Samuel J., and Amna Khalid. "Are Colleges and Universities Too Liberal? What the Research Says about the Political Composition of Campuses and Campus Climate | American Enterprise Institute - AEI." AEI, October 21, 2020. https://www.aei.org/articles/are-colleges-and-universities-too-liberal-what-the-research-says-about-the-political-composition-of-campuses-and-campus-climate/.
12 Ibid.
13 Ibid.
14 Ibid.
15 Alonso, Johanna. "Men and White People Vote Differently Based on Education." Inside Higher Ed, November 8, 2024. https://www.insidehighered.com/news/government/politics-elections/2024/11/08/men-and-white-people-vote-differently-based-education.

CHAPTER 1: THE ANCIENT CASE FOR COLLEGE

1   Hall, Edwin. The shorter catechism of the Westminster assembly, with analysis and scripture proofs. Philadelphia Presbyterian Publication Committee, 1859. Pdf. https://www.loc.gov/item/unk83002289/.
2   Denman, Mariatte, ed. "The Socratic Method: What It Is and How to Use It in the Classroom." Stanford University, 2003. https://web.archive.org/web/20220511021023/https://tomprof.stanford.edu/posting/810.
3   Kraut, Richard. "Plato." Stanford Encyclopedia of Philosophy, February 12, 2022. https://plato.stanford.edu/entries/plato/.
4   Robertson, Donald. "David Fideler: A Short History of Plato's Academy." Plato's Academy Centre, June 7, 2021. https://platosacademy.org/a-short-history-of-platos-academy/.
5   Ibid.
6   Ibid.
7   Ibid.
8   Ibid.
9   Ibid.
10 Shields, Christopher. "Aristotle." Stanford Encyclopedia of Philosophy, August 25, 2020. https://plato.stanford.edu/entries/aristotle/.

11   Ibid.
12   Kraut, Richard. "Plato." Stanford Encyclopedia of Philosophy, February 12, 2022. https://plato.stanford.edu/entries/plato/.
13   Shields, Christopher. "Aristotle." Stanford Encyclopedia of Philosophy, August 25, 2020. https://plato.stanford.edu/entries/aristotle/.
14   Ibid.
15   Morison, William. "The Lyceum." Internet encyclopedia of philosophy. Accessed September 7, 2025. https://iep.utm.edu/lyceum/.
16   Falk, Seb. The Light Ages: The Surprising Story of Medieval Science. United States: W. W. Norton, 2020.
17   Ibid.
18   Ibid.
19   Norman, Jeremy. "Foundation of the Schola Medical Salernitana, the First Western Medical School : History of Information." HistoryofInformation.com. Accessed September 8, 2025. https://historyofinformation.com/detail.php?id=3113.
20   "Our History - University of Bologna." University of Bologna. Accessed September 7, 2025. https://www.unibo.it/en/university/who-we-are/our-history.
21   "Nine Centuries of History - University of Bologna." University of Bologna. Accessed September 7, 2025. https://www.unibo.it/en/university/who-we-are/our-history/nine-centuries-of-history/nine-centuries-of-history.
22   Ibid.
23   Falk, Seb. The Light Ages: The Surprising Story of Medieval Science. United States: W. W. Norton, 2020.
24   Ibid.
25   Ibid.
26   "The Medieval University." University of Delaware British Literature Wiki. Accessed September 7, 2025. https://sites.udel.edu/britlitwiki/the-medieval-university/.
27   Falk, Seb. The Light Ages: The Surprising Story of Medieval Science. United States: W. W. Norton, 2020.
28   Ibid.
29   Ibid.
30   The Trivium: The Liberal Arts of Logic, Grammar, and Rhetoric. United States: Paul Dry Books, (n.d.).
31   Ibid.

CHAPTER 2: LATE-STAGE EDUCATION AND THE DECLINE AND FALL OF THE ELITE UNIVERSITY

1   Ryan, Delphine. "The Prussian Model of Education." STEMiteracy. Accessed September 7, 2025. https://www.stemiteracy.org/the-

prussian-model.
2. Ibid.
3. Rothbard, Murray. "Prussia." Mises Institute. Accessed September 7, 2025. https://mises.org/online-book/education-free-and-compulsory/compulsory-education-europe/prussia.
4. Ibid.
5. Ibid.
6. Ibid.
7. Ibid.
8. Ibid.
9. Ibid.
10. Ibid.
11. Johnson, Paul. Intellectuals. Japan: Harper & Row, 1988.
12. Ibid.
13. Ibid.
14. Ibid.
15. Ibid.
16. Ibid.
17. Ibid.
18. Ibid.
19. Marx, Karl. "Wild Songs by Karl Marx." Translated by Alex Miller, Diana Miller, and Victor Schnittke. Marxists Internet Archive. Accessed September 8, 2025. https://marxists.architexturez.net/archive/marx/works/1837-pre/marx/1837-wil.htm.
20. Ibid.
21. Marx, Karl. "Scenes from Oulanem." Marxists Internet Archive. Accessed September 7, 2025. https://www.marxists.org/archive/marx/works/1837-pre/verse/verse21.htm.
22. Johnson, Paul. Intellectuals. Japan: Harper & Row, 1988.
23. Kengor, Paul. The Devil and Karl Marx: Communism's Long March of Death, Deception, and Infiltration. United States: Tan Books, 2020.
24. Ibid.
25. Ibid.
26. Martin, James. "Antonio Gramsci." Stanford Encyclopedia of Philosophy, January 13, 2023. https://plato.stanford.edu/entries/gramsci/.
27. Ibid.
28. Kengor, Paul. The Devil and Karl Marx: Communism's Long March of Death, Deception, and Infiltration. United States: Tan Books, 2020.
29. Gregg, Samuel. "The Most Dangerous Socialist in History - the Stream." The Stream, July 25, 2016. https://stream.org/dangerous-marxist/.
30. Ibid.
31. Martin, James. "Antonio Gramsci." Stanford Encyclopedia of Philosophy, January 13, 2023. https://plato.stanford.edu/entries/

32 Farr, Arnold. "Herbert Marcuse." Stanford Encyclopedia of Philosophy, January 10, 2025. https://plato.stanford.edu/entries/marcuse/.
33 Ibid.
34 Marcuse, Herbert. "An Essay on Liberation." Marxists Internet Archive. Accessed September 8, 2025. https://www.marxists.org/reference/archive/marcuse/works/1969/essay-liberation.pdf.
35 Farr, Arnold. "Herbert Marcuse." Stanford Encyclopedia of Philosophy, January 10, 2025. https://plato.stanford.edu/entries/marcuse/.
36 Marcuse, Herbert. "Repressive Tolerance (Full Text)." Herbert Marcuse Official Website, 2015. https://www.marcuse.org/herbert/publications/1960s/1965-repressive-tolerance-fulltext.html.
37 Ibid.
38 Ibid.
39 Ibid.
40 Díaz, Kim. "Paulo Friere (1921-1997)." Internet encyclopedia of philosophy. Accessed September 7, 2025. https://iep.utm.edu/freire/.
41 Ibid.
42 Ibid.
43 Freire Institute. "Paulo Freire." Freire Institute. Accessed September 7, 2025. https://www.freire.org/paulo-freire/.
44 Díaz, Kim. "Paulo Friere (1921-1997)." Internet encyclopedia of philosophy. Accessed September 7, 2025. https://iep.utm.edu/freire/.
45 Ibid.
46 Ibid.
47 Shields, Jon A. "The Disappearing Conservative Professor." National Affairs, 2018. https://nationalaffairs.com/publications/detail/the-disappearing-conservative-professor.
48 Abrams, Samuel J. "The Slowing of Higher Education's Liberal Slide." AEI, March 19, 2019. https://www.aei.org/articles/the-slowing-of-higher-educations-liberal-slide/.
49 "Faculty Faith." Harvard Magazine, July 1, 2007. https://www.harvardmagazine.com/2007/07/faculty-faith-html.
50 Lipka, Michael, Patricia Tevington, and Kelsey Jo Starr. "8 Facts about Atheists." Pew Research Center, February 7, 2024. https://www.pewresearch.org/short-reads/2024/02/07/8-facts-about-atheists/.

CHAPTER 3: WHAT HAPPENS WHEN CONSERVATIVE STUDENTS GET A LIBERAL EDUCATION

1 Prov. 22:6 (KJV)
2 "Teenager Development: 13 to 18 Years (Adolescent)." Children's

3   Hospital of Orange County, June 2021. https://choc.org/ages-stages/13-to-18-years/.
3   Jarrett, Christian. "How Our Teenage Years Shape Our Personalities." BBC News, June 11, 2018. https://www.bbc.com/future/article/20180608-how-our-teenage-years-shape-our-personalities.
4   Borghuis, Jeroen, Jaap J. Denissen, Daniel Oberski, Klaas Sijtsma, Wim H. Meeus, Susan Branje, Hans M. Koot, and Wiebke Bleidorn. "Big Five Personality Stability, Change, and Codevelopment across Adolescence and Early Adulthood." Journal of Personality and Social Psychology 113, no. 4 (October 2017): 641–57. https://doi.org/10.1037/pspp0000138.
5   Sharma, Sushil, Arain, Mathur, Rais, Nel, Sandhu, Haque, and Johal. "Maturation of the Adolescent Brain." Neuropsychiatric Disease and Treatment, April 2013, 449. https://doi.org/10.2147/ndt.s39776.
6   "A Wider Ideological Gap between More and Less Educated Adults." Pew Research Center, April 26, 2016. https://www.pewresearch.org/politics/2016/04/26/a-wider-ideological-gap-between-more-and-less-educated-adults/.
7   Ibid.
8   Ibid.
9   Ibid.
10 Clark, Cullum. "Deep-Blue Birth Dearth." City Journal, July 16, 2024. https://www.city-journal.org/article/deep-blue-birth-dearth.
11 Leparmentier, Arnaud. "Elon Musk's Ambition: Repopulating the Planet and 'Destroying the Woke Virus.'" Le Monde, August 13, 2024. https://www.lemonde.fr/en/international/article/2024/08/13/elon-musk-s-ambition-repopulating-the-planet-and-destroying-the-woke-virus_6714239_4.html.
12 Peterson, Jordan B. "On Whale Carcasses." Jordan B Peterson, March 22, 2024. https://www.jordanbpeterson.com/blog/on-whale-carcasses/.
13 Ibid.

CHAPTER 4: HOW THE COLLEGE-TO-CAREER PIPELINE BROKE

1   "Sociologists." U.S. Bureau of Labor Statistics, August 28, 2025. https://www.bls.gov/ooh/life-physical-and-social-science/sociologists.htm.
2   "Room for Progress in College Graduates' Transition to the Labor Market." Public Policy Institute of California. Accessed September 8, 2025. https://www.ppic.org/blog/room-for-progress-in-college-graduates-transition-to-the-labor-market/ /
3   Ibid.
4   Ibid.
5   Ibid.

6   Hanson, Andrew, Carlo Salerno, Matt Sigelman, Mels de Zeeuw, and Stephen Moret. "Talent Disrupted: College Graduates, Underemployment, and the Way Forward." Strada Education Foundation, February 22, 2024. https://www.burningglassinstitute.org/research/underemployment.
7   Ibid.
8   Murray, Jeff. "Most College Graduates Face Underemployment upon Bachelor's Degree Attainment." Thomas B. Fordham Institute, March 7, 2024. https://fordhaminstitute.org/national/commentary/most-college-graduates-face-underemployment-upon-bachelors-degree-attainment.
9   Hanson, Andrew, Carlo Salerno, Matt Sigelman, Mels de Zeeuw, and Stephen Moret. "Talent Disrupted: College Graduates, Underemployment, and the Way Forward." Strada Education Foundation, February 22, 2024. https://www.burningglassinstitute.org/research/underemployment.
10 Busteed, Brandon. "Higher Education's Work Preparation Paradox." Gallup.com, February 25, 2014. https://news.gallup.com/opinion/gallup/173249/higher-education-work-preparation-paradox.aspx.
11 Ibid.
12 Ibid.
13 Ibid.
14 Ibid.
15 DiNino, Lance. "Death By a Thousand Emails: How Administrative Bloat Is Killing American Higher Education." The Bowdoin Review, February 7, 2024. https://students.bowdoin.edu/bowdoin-review/features/death-by-a-thousand-emails-how-administrative-bloat-is-killing-american-higher-education/.
16 Weinstein, Paul. "Administrative Bloat at U.S. Colleges Is Skyrocketing." Forbes, August 28, 2022. https://www.forbes.com/sites/paulweinstein/2023/08/28/administrative-bloat-at-us-colleges-is-skyrocketing/.
17 Wood, Sarah. "See the Average College Tuition in 2024-2025." US News & World Report, September 26, 2024. https://www.usnews.com/education/best-colleges/paying-for-college/articles/paying-for-college-infographic.
18 Fry, Richard, and Anthony Cilluffo. "5 Facts about Student Loans." Pew Research Center, September 18, 2024. https://www.pewresearch.org/short-reads/2024/09/18/facts-about-student-loans/.

CHAPTER 5: HOW UNIVERSITIES CAN DO BETTER

1   Guinness, Os. "Our Civilisational Moment." ARC Research, February 20, 2024. https://www.arc-research.org/research-papers/our-civilisational-moment.

2   Ibid.
3   Ibid.
4   Ibid.
5   Fry, Richard, and Anthony Cilluffo. "5 Facts about Student Loans." Pew Research Center, September 18, 2024. https://www.pewresearch.org/short-reads/2024/09/18/facts-about-student-loans/.
6   Wood, Sarah. "See the Average College Tuition in 2024-2025." US News & World Report, September 26, 2024. https://www.usnews.com/education/best-colleges/paying-for-college/articles/paying-for-college-infographic.
7   Ibid.
8   Thompson, Mary. "Crowdfunding College and Other Clever Ways to Cut Costs." CNBC, August 30, 2013. https://www.cnbc.com/2013/08/30/crowdfunding-college-and-other-clever-ways-to-cut-costs.html.
9   "Nearly 4 in 10 Employers Avoid Hiring Recent College Grads in Favor of Older Workers." Intelligent, December 12, 2023. https://www.intelligent.com/nearly-4-in-10-employers-avoid-hiring-recent-college-grads-in-favor-of-older-workers/.
10 "The Best Job Hunting Resources You Should Be Taking Advantage Of." UEI College, May 26, 2017. https://www.uei.edu/blog/the-best-job-hunting-resources-you-should-be-taking-advantage-of/.
11 "Why You Should Visit Your College's Career Center." CollegeData. Accessed September 7, 2025. https://www.collegedata.com/college-to-career/why-you-should-visit-your-colleges-career-center.
12 "St. John's Reading List: A Great Books Curriculum." St. John's College. Accessed September 7, 2025. https://www.sjc.edu/academic-programs/undergraduate/great-books-reading-list.

CHAPTER 6: HOW TO PREPARE FOR COLLEGE LONG BEFORE COLLEGE

1   "Office for Civil Rights Initiates Title VI Investigations into Institutions of Higher Education." U.S. Department of Education, March 14, 2025. https://www.ed.gov/about/news/press-release/office-civil-rights-initiates-title-vi-investigations-institutions-of-higher-education-0.
2   Johnson, Reece. "New Survey Finds Most College Grads Would Change Majors: BestColleges." BestColleges, March 20, 2023. https://www.bestcolleges.com/blog/college-graduate-majors-survey/.

CHAPTER 7: GETTING EVERYTHING WE CAN OUT OF THE COLLEGE EXPERIENCE

1   "Mental Health Issues on the Rise Among College Students Post-Pandemic." Wiley, March 11, 2024. https://johnwiley2020news.q4web.com/press-releases/press-release-details/2024/Mental-Health-Issues-on-the-Rise-Among-College-Students-Post-Pandemic/.

2 Zhai, Yusen, and Xue Du. "Trends in Diagnosed Posttraumatic Stress Disorder and Acute Stress Disorder in US College Students, 2017-2022." JAMA Network Open 7, no. 5 (May 30, 2024). https://doi.org/10.1001/jamanetworkopen.2024.13874.
3 Lipson, Sarah Ketchen, Sasha Zhou, Sara Abelson, Justin Heinze, Matthew Jirsa, Jasmine Morigney, Akilah Patterson, Meghna Singh, and Daniel Eisenberg. "Trends in College Student Mental Health and Help-Seeking by Race/Ethnicity: Findings from the National Healthy Minds Study, 2013–2021." Journal of Affective Disorders 306 (June 2022): 138–47. https://doi.org/10.1016/j.jad.2022.03.038.
4 "Mental Health Issues on the Rise Among College Students Post-Pandemic." Wiley, March 11, 2024. https://johnwiley2020news.q4web.com/press-releases/press-release-details/2024/Mental-Health-Issues-on-the-Rise-Among-College-Students-Post-Pandemic/.
5 "College Student and Graduate Behavioral Health Report." United Healthcare. Accessed September 8, 2025. https://www.uhc.com/content/dam/uhcdotcom/en/HealthAndWellness/PDF/UHC-College-Student-and-Graduate-BH-Report.pdf.
6 Ibid.
7 Ibid.
8 "Mental Health Issues on the Rise Among College Students Post-Pandemic." Wiley, March 11, 2024. https://johnwiley2020news.q4web.com/press-releases/press-release-details/2024/Mental-Health-Issues-on-the-Rise-Among-College-Students-Post-Pandemic/.
9 Ibid.
10 Earls, Aaron. "Most Teenagers Drop out of Church When They Become Young Adults." Lifeway Research, January 15, 2019. https://lifewayresearch.com/2019/01/15/most-teenagers-drop-out-of-church-as-young-adults/.

CHAPTER 8: HOW TO FINISH SCHOOL STRONG AND GET A BEST FIRST REAL JOB

1 Ingle, Kent. "Why Trump's $3 Billion Wake-up Call to Higher Ed Is Exactly What America Needs." Fox News, June 6, 2025. https://www.foxnews.com/opinion/why-trumps-3-billion-wake-up-call-higher-ed-exactly-what-america-needs.
2 Rowe, Mike. "2.5 Million in Trade School Scholarships." Mike Rowe, March 1, 2025. https://mikerowe.com/2025/03/2-5-million-in-trade-school-scholarships/.
3 https://seu.edu/academics/seu-trades/

CHAPTER 10: THE TRUTH ABOUT THE TRADES, ASSOCIATE'S DEGREES, AND PROFESSIONAL CERTIFICATIONS

1 Sidoti, Olivia, Eugenie Park, and Jeffrey Gottfried. "About a Quarter of U.S. Teens Have Used CHATGPT for Schoolwork – Double the

Share in 2023." Pew Research Center, January 15, 2025. https://www.pewresearch.org/short-reads/2025/01/15/about-a-quarter-of-us-teens-have-used-chatgpt-for-schoolwork-double-the-share-in-2023/.
2. Walsh, James D. "Everyone Is Cheating Their Way through College." Intelligencer, May 7, 2025. https://nymag.com/intelligencer/article/openai-chatgpt-ai-cheating-education-college-students-school.html.
3. Camp, Emma. "Why Are Students Using AI To Cheat? Maybe Because They Shouldn't Be In College At All." Reason, July 18, 2025. https://reason.com/2025/07/18/why-are-students-using-ai-to-cheat-maybe-because-they-shouldnt-be-in-college-at-all/.
4. Ibid.
5. Lin, Luona. "A Quarter of U.S. Teachers Say AI Tools Do More Harm than Good in K-12 Education." Pew Research Center, May 15, 2024. https://www.pewresearch.org/short-reads/2024/05/15/a-quarter-of-u-s-teachers-say-ai-tools-do-more-harm-than-good-in-k-12-education/.
6. "Teaching for Tomorrow: Unlocking Six Weeks a Year With AI." Gallup, 2025. https://www.gallup.com/analytics/659819/k-12-teacher-research.aspx.
7. "Vibe Coding Explained: Tools and Guides." Google Cloud. Accessed September 8, 2025. https://cloud.google.com/discover/what-is-vibe-coding.
8. Replit. Accessed September 8, 2025. https://replit.com/.
9. Nolan, Beatrice. "AI-Powered Coding Tool Wiped out a Software Company's Database in 'Catastrophic Failure.'" Fortune, July 23, 2025. https://fortune.com/2025/07/23/ai-coding-tool-replit-wiped-database-called-it-a-catastrophic-failure/.
10. Ibid.
11. Ibid.
12. Lyon, Christopher F. "Fake Cases, Real Consequences: Misuse of ChatGPT Leads to Sanctions." Goldberg Segalla, 2023. https://www.goldbergsegalla.com/app/uploads/2023/10/Fake-Cases-Real-Consequences-Misuse-of-ChatGPT-Christoper-F.-Lyon-NY-Litigator.pdf.
13. Ibid.
14. Ibid.
15. Ibid.
16. Volokh, Eugene. "Lawyer Explains How He Used ChatGPT to Produce Filing 'Replete with Citations to Non-Existent Cases.'" Reason.com, July 7, 2023. https://reason.com/volokh/2023/06/07/lawyer-explains-how-he-used-chatgpt-to-produce-filing-replete-with-citations-to-non-existent-cases/.
17. Ibid.
18. "What Is Machine Learning (ML) ?" IBM. Accessed September 8, 2025. https://www.ibm.com/think/topics/machine-learning.

19 Caballar, Rina Dianne. "Generative AI vs. Predictive Ai: What's the Difference?" IBM, August 9, 2024. https://www.ibm.com/think/topics/generative-ai-vs-predictive-ai-whats-the-difference.
20 Ibid.
21 "What Is a Large Language Model (LLM)?" Cloudflare. Accessed September 8, 2025. https://www.cloudflare.com/learning/ai/what-is-large-language-model/.
22 Burtell, Matthew, and Helen Toner. "The Surprising Power of Next Word Prediction: Large Language Models Explained, Part 1." CSET, March 8, 2024. https://cset.georgetown.edu/article/the-surprising-power-of-next-word-prediction-large-language-models-explained-part-1/.
23 "What Is a Stochastic Parrot?" Moveworks. Accessed September 8, 2025. https://www.moveworks.com/us/en/resources/ai-terms-glossary/stochastic-parrot.
24 "What Are AI Hallucinations?" Cloudflare. Accessed September 8, 2025. https://www.cloudflare.com/learning/ai/what-are-ai-hallucinations/.
25 Ibid.

CHAPTER 11: AI AND THE FUTURE OF EDUCATION

1 Prov. 31:26 (KJV)
2 Jury, Karen. "Well-Behaved Women Seldom Make History: Quotes and Context for Women's History Month." Library blog - LibGuides at Central Penn College, March 29, 2022. https://guides.centralpenn.edu/blog/Well-Behaved-Women-Seldom-Make-History-Quotes-and-Context-for-Womens-History-Month.
3 Hernandez, Donald J., and Jeffrey S. Napierala. "Mother's Education and Children's Outcomes: How Dual-Generation Programs Offer Increased Opportunities for America's Families." Foundation For Child Development, July 9, 2014. https://www.fcd-us.org/wp-content/uploads/2016/04/Mothers-Education-and-Childrens-Outcomes-FINAL.pdf.
4 Ibid.
5 Ibid.
6 "Single Mothers with College Degrees Much Less Likely to Live in Poverty." IWPR, July 2018. https://iwpr.org/wp-content/uploads/2020/08/Q072_Single-Mothers-College-Degrees-Poverty-1.pdf.

www.ingramcontent.com/pod-product-compliance
Lightning Source LLC
Chambersburg PA
CBHW022058120526
44580CB00017B/127/J